Maturing assets

The evolution of stock transfer housing associations

Hal Pawson and Cathie Fancy

The POLICY PRESS

First published in Great Britain in September 2003 by

The Policy Press
Fourth Floor, Beacon House
Queen's Road
Bristol BS8 1QU
UK

Tel no +44 (0)117 331 4054
Fax no +44 (0)117 331 4093
E-mail tpp-info@bristol.ac.uk
www.policypress.org.uk

© Heriot-Watt University 2003

Published for the Joseph Rowntree Foundation by The Policy Press

ISBN 1 86134 545 3

Hal Pawson is Senior Research Fellow and **Cathie Fancy** is Research Associate, both in the School of the Built Environment, Heriot-Watt University, Edinburgh.

The **Joseph Rowntree Foundation** has supported this project as part of its programme of research and innovative development projects, which it hopes will be of value to policy makers, practitioners and service users. The facts presented and views expressed in this report are, however, those of the authors and not necessarily those of the Foundation.

The statements and opinions contained within this publication are solely those of the authors and not of The University of Bristol or The Policy Press. The University of Bristol and The Policy Press disclaim responsibility for any injury to persons or property resulting from any material published in this publication.

The Policy Press works to counter discrimination on grounds of gender, race, disability, age and sexuality.

Cover design by Qube Design Associates, Bristol
Printed in Great Britain by Hobbs the Printers Ltd, Southampton

Contents

List of tables and figures

Tables

Figures

Acknowledgements

This study has been made possible mainly by the generous help provided by numerous managers, staff and board members of the stock transfer housing associations selected as case studies. We are also indebted to the 61 transfer housing association chief executives and senior colleagues who completed our postal survey questionnaire and to representatives of national stakeholder organisations who kindly agreed to be interviewed. Thanks are also due to The Housing Corporation and Communities Scotland for allowing us access to regulatory statistical data.

The research also benefited from the guidance provided by its Advisory Group, kindly facilitated and resourced by the Joseph Rowntree Foundation. We are grateful for the help provided in this context by **Danny Burns, Dr Cathy Davis, John Keyes, Theresa McDonagh, Peter Malpass, Peter Marcus, Claire Miller, David Mullins, Ian Nagle, Dr Barbara Reid, Ian Swift** and **Peter Westley**.

Thanks are due to **Madhu Satsangi**, our Heriot-Watt University colleague who carried out some of the case study fieldwork. And **Professor Moira Munro** played a key role in the project's genesis and helped to shape its ongoing development.

Executive summary

Introduction

In the past 15 years, social housing in Britain has been substantially restructured through the transfer of former council stock to housing association (HA) ownership. HAs now manage over a third of all social sector dwellings – a threefold increase on the proportion in 1991.

Since the transfer process began in earnest in the late 1980s, more than 870,000 (tenanted) homes have been passed from state ownership (that is, local authorities [LAs], New Town development corporations or Scottish Homes) to housing associations. By early 2003, 111 LAs in England had transferred all their stock to HAs. Taking account of local government reorganisation, this left 109 of England's 354 LAs as 'post-transfer' councils – that is, with no landlord role. In addition, over 40 LAs (23 in England and 19 in Scotland) have carried out partial stock transfers – that is, where a council disposes of a package of tenanted housing while also retaining stock in its ownership.

The establishment of new social landlords

The vast majority of transferred stock has been taken into ownership by newly created – rather than existing – HAs. In most cases these have been set up as freestanding bodies, although a few were established as subsidiaries of existing associations. In all, therefore, the transfer process has spawned over 180 'transfer landlords' (or 'transfer associations'), which now account for almost half of total HA stock.

Given central government's continuing policy commitment to the active promotion of transfers

and the established tendency to set up new landlord bodies for this purpose, it is likely that such organisations will come to dominate the entire social housing sector by the end of the present decade. It is these agencies which form the subject of this report.

Research scope and methodology

Covering both England and Scotland, the research focused in particular on transfer landlords created before 1 April 1999. It encompassed organisations created through transfers from LAs and from Scottish Homes. The study involved four main elements:

- interviews with national stakeholder agencies;
- analysis of regulatory and other secondary data;
- a postal survey of transfer landlords;
- case studies focusing on 12 transfer landlords.

Transfer motivations and processes

Particularly in their early existence, the structures and operation of transfer HAs are often attributable to the motivations which inspired their creation or to aspects of the policy framework prevailing at transfer. Significant influence is also often wielded by consultants brought in to advise on the creation of the new landlord bodies. By far the most important factor stimulating 'bottom-up' interest in transfer has been the scope for HAs to fund the refurbishment of ex-LA (or Scottish Homes) stock through their privileged access to private finance. In certain local instances, other motivations – such as boosting the supply of new affordable housing – have been important. As well as exerting a critical influence on the governance structures established within the new landlords, registration criteria for new HAs (as operated by The Housing Corporation and by Communities Scotland) have significantly impacted on recruitment procedures and the adoption of formal housing management policies.

Organisational structures

Even on Day 1, the structure of newly established transfer HAs typically differs substantially from that of pre-transfer housing services. While most of their staff may be inherited from the predecessor landlord, many will have been located outside the department primarily responsible for housing. Consultants' models have tended to generate a degree of uniformity across the sector in terms of transfer HA organisational structures.

The tendency for transfer HAs to operate with less hierarchical structures than predecessor landlords is common, although not universal. Flatter configurations are generally preferred because they are seen as consistent with empowering staff and devolving managerial responsibility. Such changes are generally seen as having followed directly from the switch from LA (or Scottish Homes) to HA status rather than simply reflecting ongoing trends affecting social landlords across the board.

There has been a common tendency among transfer HAs for early experimentation with more generic approaches – initiatives often subsequently rolled back. Growing specialisation is associated with increasing centralisation with the main driver being the overriding emphasis on maximising rent collection to meet business plan income targets.

Most partial transfer HAs have been created as 'group subsidiaries', and the majority of whole stock transfer HAs have looked into or proceeded with setting up group structures since their creation. By 2002, only a minority of whole stock transfer HAs remained as 'freestanding' unitary organisations. Particularly where they involve the possibility of collaboration with another landlord, deliberations over the creation of group structures have substantial potential for

causing conflict within transfer HA boards and between HAs and their LA partners. However, many group structures operated by transfer HAs are of the 'internal group' type (that is, not involving collaboration with other previously independent HAs) and this kind of arrangement is less contentious.

Staff management and organisational culture

Transfer HAs overwhelmingly see their exposure to risk as changing the balance between business and social imperatives, as compared with predecessor organisations. There is a common managerial emphasis on securing widespread employee ownership of business plan objectives and targets. This is widely successful and forms an essential foundation for the development of a performance culture.

Generally, staff confirm managerial assertions that, by comparison with predecessor organisations, transfer HAs value their employees highly and that there is a greater corporate emphasis on staff training. From the viewpoint of transferring staff, the post-transfer regime is widely seen as replacing a bureaucratic, hierarchical work environment with one that is more egalitarian, inclusive and encouraging of initiative.

While transfer HAs are increasingly moving away from linkage with the annual LA pay round, and some have experimented with 'private sector' approaches such as performance-related pay, there is no clear trend towards the more widespread adoption of mechanisms of this kind.

Transfer HAs generally aspire to operate in a more consumerist way than their predecessor landlords and the limited evidence available suggests that this ambition is realised at least to some extent.

Corporate governance

Particularly in England, transfer HAs stand out as distinct from their 'traditional' HA counterparts in that their management boards typically involve substantial tenant and council nominee (usually councillor) representation. Among English transfer HAs there are signs of a limited tendency for reducing councillor board representation, in some cases in favour of an increased tenant presence.

By comparison with the other main 'constituency' groups, councillor board participation lacks stability and continuity. This restricts the scope for the accumulation of knowledge and experience and, therefore, limits the typical value of councillor board input. Particularly in a transfer HA's early days, it is not unusual for councillors to be seen as attempting to wield influence and conduct meetings in inappropriate ways. In part, this can reflect a mistaken belief that the new body is susceptible to council direction and control.

While their attendance record is typically good, there are widespread concerns that tenant board members do not always play a full part in board decision making. In spite of a frequently substantial HA commitment to board member training, there is a fairly common HA staff perception of tenant board members playing a 'silent partner' role or fully engaging only with day-to-day operational issues (rather than more strategic matters).

'Independent' board members, often recruited from legal, property or financial fields, are typically more long-serving than either council or tenant board members. Their 'non-political' approach and specialist knowledge are often seen as 'refreshing' by transfer HA chief executives. Whilst independent board members were, at one time, often recruited in a fairly ad hoc way, many transfer HAs (like the larger of their traditional HA counterparts) are now moving towards formal advertising and interview selection systems.

In the evolution of board operation, initial factionalism tends to die away over time – although this 'coming together' process is sometimes stimulated by regulatory intervention or advice.

Housing management

In general, the switch to HA status involves the adoption of a wide range of documented policies to comply with the formal regulation operated in the HA sector. Actual policy changes are, in many cases, symptomatic of moves towards a more 'customer-focused' style of operation. As far as the balance between business and social objectives is concerned, transfer HAs tend to see themselves as operating 'tighter' but not necessarily 'tougher' approaches – for example in managing rent arrears.

In terms of their propensity to evict tenants, there is no justification for the hypothesis that transfer HAs are habitually tough landlords by comparison with LAs or with other HAs. Indeed, transfer HAs' eviction rates are well below those of these other classes of social landlord.

Stakeholder views chime with previous research evidence showing that housing management performance (and average tenant satisfaction) tends to improve following stock transfer. There is, however, no clear evidence for the belief that transfer HAs, as a class of landlords, outperform comparable LAs. While transfer landlords may be more tenant-influenced, tenant-friendly and consumerist in outlook, it is not clear that they are generally 'higher performing' housing managers than LAs. Within the HA sector, nevertheless, they set standards which others struggle to match.

Finance and development

Particularly in their early years, transfer HAs' highly indebted status and their need to honour often very specific 'transfer promises' makes them extremely vulnerable to unforeseen changes in the economic or regulatory environment. This can impose substantial pressures on inexperienced management boards, sometimes necessitating regulator intervention.

While the need to re-invest in existing housing is the main motivation for most stock transfers, virtually all transfer HAs in England – and most in Scotland – are also active developers of new housing. Around half the transfer landlords in England have been contractually required to develop new homes through clauses in transfer agreements. Collectively, transfer HAs have built around 50,000 homes since 1988 – of which around 80% have been social rented dwellings.

Nevertheless, transfer HAs' annual stock losses (mainly through Right to Buy [RTB] sales and, to a lesser extent, demolitions) considerably exceed stock expansion through acquisition and development. Hence, more than two thirds of transfer landlords have seen their stock decline in net terms since set-up. Even among the longest-established organisations this is true of nearly half. Seven per cent of transfer landlords in England and a quarter in Scotland have seen total stock contract by more than 10%.

As well as being a response to the requirements of founding LAs, transfer HAs' 'development drive' usually reflects internal motivations, especially the perceived need to counteract ongoing post-transfer stock losses (mainly due to the effect of RTB sales). The aim here is to counteract rising unit management costs due to central overheads being spread across declining stock numbers. Another factor relevant to landlords emerging from the intensive stock refurbishment phase following transfer, may be the wish to capitalise on the development expertise accumulated through this process.

Around 60% of English pre-1999 transfer HAs have developed housing outside the boundaries of their original 'home LA'. A relatively large proportion of such schemes involve Low Cost Home Ownership or market renting rather than social rented housing. While 'out of area' development amounts to 44% of all new homes built by transfer HAs, this is strongly influenced by the activities of 'early cohort' landlords mainly in the first half of the 1990s. Few of the more recently set up associations in England (and virtually none in Scotland) anticipate 'out of area' development on any scale in the foreseeable future. It is therefore highly unlikely that many of these bodies will quickly develop into major regional players as some of their 'first-wave' counterparts have done. Both external circumstances and internal governance arrangements are influential here.

Many transfer HAs are pursuing 'functional diversification', either in terms of activities under the 'community regeneration' heading, or involvement in non-housing pursuits seen as attractive in purely business terms. Most English transfer HAs have developed community facilities and/or provided training, money advice or community development input for neighbourhoods where they have a major

landlord presence. In some cases – primarily among more recently set up associations – such moves reflect the requirements of founding LAs. In others they may reflect the drive to 'grow the business' to counteract stock attrition.

Relationships between transfer HAs and LAs

The great majority of transfer associations set up in England believe that they have a 'special relationship' with their founding LA. In Scotland, where most transfer landlords have a different origin and where local authorities have never had a role in funding HA development, such links are much less common.

In part, an ongoing special relationship between a transfer HA and its founding LA is often attributable to a persisting sense of 'ownership' on the council's part as well as to the association's typical dominance of the local social housing scene in purely numerical terms. Other important factors frequently include continuing functional integration between the parties. This can involve transfer HAs playing a contractor role in the provision of services to the council and/or buying services from the council.

Tensions, however, often attend the LA/transfer HA relationship. Some of these are day-to-day operational issues, different only in scale from those common to relationships between LAs and traditional HAs. Others, however, are quite distinct, and mark out the interaction between transfer HAs and their LA partners as being different in kind to that involving LAs and non-transfer associations. While these include operational issues resulting from functional integration, others are more strategic in nature. In particular, a transfer HA's attempts to counter unforeseen budgetary problems (for example by centralising services or contemplating a merger with another HA) may attract strongly expressed concerns on the part of a founder LA where such plans are seen as contravening pre-transfer undertakings.

Stresses between transfer HAs and founding LAs are often at their most acute during the immediate post-transfer period, as both parties adjust to their respective roles under the new regime. As far as longer-term changes are concerned, only a third of English transfer HAs believe that their relationship with their home LA has subsequently become more distant than in the immediate post-transfer period. In Scotland, where most such relationships admittedly start from a low base, most transfer HAs see themselves as having moved at least somewhat closer to their respective home LAs.

Conclusions

Since the late 1980s, stock transfer has been a catalyst for substantial change in the delivery of social housing services and in the management of social housing organisations. In part, this reflects the ability of transfer associations – properly set up – to access investment resources, but also derives from the fact that the post-transfer regime has tended to result in:

- a liberating effect on housing staff;
- the adoption of a more customer-focused approach to housing management;
- innovations in landlords' organisational structures and staff management practices in favour of more openness and more widespread ownership of corporate objectives.

Alongside such changes, transfer often triggers genuine transformation in organisational ethos – summarised by staff interviewees in some of our case studies as replacing a 'no' culture with a 'yes' culture.

Partly due to their need to accommodate common regulatory requirements, transfer landlords inevitably develop some similarities with 'traditional housing associations'. Collectively, however, transfer HAs retain a number of distinctive features, for example:

- a stock profile which, in age, type and design, differs from that of most traditional associations;
- particularly close ties with founder LAs, either through functional integration, through 'preferred development partner' status or through the influence wielded at board level by councillor board members;

- substantial tenant participation[1] in governance (contrasting less significantly with traditional associations in Scotland than in England);
- a local focus to their activities differing from that of non-transfer associations of a comparable size;
- a growth imperative resulting from the contraction of stock due to the continuing impact of RTB sales;
- a longer-term potential to generate substantial surpluses which may be ploughed back into additional housing development or into non-housing 'community regeneration' style activities.

A number of these distinctive features are likely to remain present for the foreseeable future.

At the same time, there is considerable differentiation within the transfer HA sub-sector. More recently created organisations are generally operating from a less favourable base and will perhaps always have less scope than the most fortunate older organisations. Similarly, with prospective changes in the transfer regime (for example, affecting stock valuations and the balance of advantage between partial and whole stock transfers) the newly created transfer landlords of the future may have different prospects from their longer-established counterparts.

---

[1] Although not necessarily substantial influence over organisational governance.

Introduction

The stock transfer phenomenon

In the past 20 years, social housing in Britain has contracted by some 25%, largely due to the sale of former council-owned dwellings to sitting tenants. By 2001, the combined stock of councils (or LAs) and HAs had shrunk to 21% of all dwellings; down from 32% in 1981 (ODPM, 2002). At the same time, however, the composition of the sector has been substantially restructured, mainly through the transfer of former council stock into HA ownership. HAs now manage more than a third of all social sector dwellings (see Table 1).

Since the transfer process began in earnest in the late 1980s, more than 870,000 (tenanted) homes have been passed from state ownership (that is, LAs, New Town development corporations or Scottish Homes) to HAs. By early 2003, 111 LAs in England had transferred all their stock to HAs – see Table 2. Taking account of local government reorganisation, this left 109 of England's 354 LAs as 'post-transfer' councils – that is, with no landlord role.

Over 40 LAs (23 in England and 19 in Scotland) have carried out partial stock transfers – that is,

where a council disposes of a package of tenanted housing while also retaining stock in its ownership. A number of authorities have made successive partial transfers usually involving individual estates or groups of estates. Glasgow City Council, for instance, made 76 transfers of this kind before handing over its entire remaining stock to Glasgow HA. Three English partial transfers have involved stock defined by type – sheltered housing – rather than by geographical location. An additional transfer variant, pioneered by Sunderland Metropolitan Borough Council (MBC) in 2001, involved a two-stage transfer, with council stock being passed initially to a city-wide HA and then subsequently to a constellation of locally based associations across the authority. Glasgow HA plans a similar process, albeit over a number of years.

The establishment of new social landlords

As Table 3 illustrates, the vast majority of transferred stock has been taken into ownership by newly created – rather than existing – HAs. In most cases these have been set up as freestanding bodies, although 17 were established as subsidiaries of existing associations. In all, therefore, the transfer

Table 1: Estimated breakdown of social rented stock, March 2003

	LA	Transfer HAs	Non-transfer HAs	Total
England	63.6	16.9	19.5	100.0
Scotland	62.5	20.5	17.0	100.0
England and Scotland	63.5	17.4	19.1	100.0

Note: Figures for Scotland exclude residual Scottish Homes stock.

Source: Authors' estimates based on dwelling stock at 31 March 2002, taking account of subsequent transfers. 2002 dwelling stock figures from ODPM (2002)

Table 2: Stock transfers since 1988 in England and Scotland: breakdown of transfer transactions by transfer type

	England			Scotland			Total
	LA whole stock	LA partial	LA whole stock	LA partial	Scottish Homes	New Towns	England & Scotland
Number of transfers	111	49	3	142	160	15	480
Dwellings transferred	634,000	72,000	93,000	19,000	49,000	4,000	871,000

Notes:

1. Number of whole stock transfers is defined as cases where a council transfers all its housing stock (irrespective of the number of HAs taking on ownership of the transferred dwellings).

2. 111 LAs undertaking whole stock transfers passed stock to 120 HAs because 9 undertook split transfers.

3. Scottish Homes transfers include 59 'Tenants Choice' and vacant possession transactions involving 2,783 homes.

4. Scottish New Town transfers exclude the 22,446 homes transferred to LAs and Scottish Homes.

5. Scottish LA transfers – stock numbers for Glasgow and Scottish Borders Councils are estimated.

Sources: England – ODPM stock transfers table (unpublished); Scotland – Taylor (1998, 2001); Communities Scotland transfers dataset (unpublished)

process has spawned over 180 'transfer landlords' (or 'transfer associations') which now account for almost half of all HA stock (see Table 3).

Despite government wishes to the contrary (Mullins et al, 1995, p 22; DETR, 2000, p 63), newly created – rather than existing – HAs have continued to dominate the stock transfer process. This has been attributed in part to predecessor landlords' preference for creating successor bodies with a degree of 'local accountability' in terms of the representation of elected councillors

(Malpass, 2000). This motivation may, in turn, be explained by "the local political judgement ... that only a new local organisation will bring the support needed for transfer both in the community generally, and in the ballot" (NHF, 2002a, p 2).

Given central government's continuing policy commitment to the active promotion of transfers and the established tendency to set up new landlord bodies for this purpose, such organisations may well come to dominate the

Table 3: Stock transfers by recipient HA type

	England		Scotland		All	
	Number of HAs	Stock transferred	Number of HAs	Stock transferred	Number of HAs	Stock transferred
Newly created HA – subsidiary within group structure	17	31,000	0	0	17	31,000
Newly created HA – freestanding	128	651,000	36	133,000	164	784,000
Total 'transfer landlords'	145	682,000	36	133,000	181	815,000
Existing HA	24	24,000	108	32,000	132	56,000
Total transfers	169	706,000	144	165,000	313	871,000

Notes:

1. English transfers relate to the 169 packages of stock transferred – see Table 2, note 2.

2. Scottish figures relate to the number of landlords involved.

3. Newly created freestanding HAs include three non-registered landlords.

4. 'Transfer landlords' in Scotland equate to Communities Scotland's 'debt-funded' peer group.

Sources: England – ODPM stock transfers table (unpublished); Scotland – Taylor (1998, 2001); Communities Scotland transfers dataset (unpublished)

entire social housing sector within the next five years. It is these agencies that form the subject of this report.

Transfer landlords within the HA sector

The transfer phenomenon has generated considerable research activity since 1990. In the main, assessments have focused on the process itself, on financial implications, and on the extent to which policy outcomes have met expectations on the part of central government and the former landlords concerned. To the extent that they have examined the impact of transfer on organisational structures, cultures and services, these studies have been generally focused on the immediate impact of the new regime. While this report is likewise concerned with the predecessor landlord/successor HA comparison, it concentrates mainly on the ways that successor bodies develop in the years following their creation.

In addition to studies on the transfer process and its outcomes, there is also a body of academic research utilising organisational management theories and concepts in an attempt to understand and map the changing nature of HAs more generally (Walker, 1998, 2000, 2001; Jacobs and Manzi, 2000; Mullins and Riseborough, 2000; Mullins et al, 2001). However, while these studies offer insights into the cultural, structural and managerial development of HAs during the 1990s, they have tended not to distinguish between transfer landlords and 'conventional HAs'. Unlike previous studies this research focuses specifically on the nature, operation and evolution of the HAs created through the transfer process.

The implicit assumption of much existing research is that there is no significant distinction between transfer associations and their 'conventional' counterparts. The Housing Corporation, as the national HA regulator in England, communicates the same message by integrating transfer landlords with others in terms of management performance 'peer groups'. Indeed, the need to work within a common regulatory framework is likely to generate considerable similarity between transfer associations and others. At the same time, however, there are a number of characteristics specific to these bodies, apart from their origins as 'offshoots' of state housing bodies, in particular:

- their typical debt profile, with an initially high level of indebtedness (resulting from the need to take out loans in order to pay for the purchase and renovation of the stock) potentially preceding the generation of substantial revenue surpluses in the medium and longer term;
- their relatively large size and the local concentration of holdings (initially, at least);
- their governance arrangements.

Research questions

The extent to which differences as listed above mark out transfer associations as a "a new breed of dynamic RSLs (Registered Social Landlords)" (Cobbold and Dean, 2000, p 6) is a key question addressed by this research. To what extent, for example, do transfer HAs fulfil an early prediction that they would 'retain the ethos of the local authority housing department, with a greater tendency towards bureaucracy coupled with a less independent tradition (than conventional housing associations)' (Cope, 1990, p 295)? What are transfer landlords' governance arrangements and how do these compare with those of 'conventional HAs'? How far have the new organisations, which generally inherit their staff from predecessor state landlords, taken on the values and ethos of the antecedent body? In addressing such questions through newly collated empirical evidence, it is hoped that light will be shed on the broader impact of stock transfer as the main driving force in the current restructuring of social housing in Britain.

Research scope and methodology

Covering both England and Scotland, the research focused in particular on transfer landlords created before 1 April 1999. It is, of course, appreciated that the changing profile of stock transfers over time means that transfer landlords created before 1999 are unlikely to be wholly representative of transfer HAs set up more recently (or, for that matter, those established in the future). In particular, more recent transfers have included a higher proportion taking place in urban contexts and involving stock in poor condition and/or affected by low demand. However, the 1999 cut-off date reflected a concern to focus on the way that transfer landlords develop and evolve over time and it was felt that those in existence for less than three years when the fieldwork was undertaken would have been too recently established for their experience to be relevant in this context.

The study covered organisations created through transfers from LAs and from Scottish Homes, although those with less than 750 homes in ownership in 2001 were excluded on the grounds that their limited staffing numbers might make it difficult for them to participate. The main consequence of this threshold was a somewhat limited representation of English partial transfer and ex-Scottish Homes transfer landlords.

The study involved four main elements:

- a postal survey of transfer landlords;
- case studies focusing on 12 transfer landlords;
- interviews with national stakeholder agencies;
- analysis of regulatory and other secondary data.

Recognising the significant differences in the institutional context between England and Scotland, two slightly differing questionnaires were used in the postal survey. The survey drew 61 responses from a total number of 106 transfer landlords, a response rate of 58%.

Postal survey respondents were eligible for possible inclusion in the case study phase. The case study HAs included nine in England and three in Scotland. These were selected to reflect the diversity of the sector in both jurisdictions (see the list of case study HAs in Table 21 in the Appendix). In particular, the cohort of case study HAs was varied in terms of:

- age/length of time since set-up;
- partial versus whole stock transfer;
- region;
- size;
- independence/involvement in group structures.

In addition, the sample included one organisation (Weslo) which is a non-registered HA where senior managers are also board members.

Case study work involved in-depth interviews with chief executives of transfer HAs, together with middle management and front-line staff in each selected organisation. These latter contacts were particularly important, given the need to ensure that research findings are not unduly influenced by the views of senior staff whose sentiments may not be wholly representative of their junior colleagues.

Each case study also involved interviews with association board members and LA housing strategy officers so as to explore their potentially contrasting perspectives. Tenants' views were probed mainly through interviews with tenant board members. Additionally, we drew on board papers, association annual reports, transfer agreements and other documents kindly provided by case study associations and their partner agencies. See the Appendix for a fuller description of the methodology for this research.

Report structure

The report now goes on to provide some background to the stock transfer process at the national level, and – drawing mainly on our case study evidence – at the local scale. The evolution of many transfer landlords is significantly influenced by the events leading to their initial establishment. Chapter 3 looks at the way that organisational structures have been set up within transfer HAs, and at how these have evolved over time. Chapter 4 examines the ways that staff management practices and other aspects of organisational culture have evolved. Chapter 5 focuses on governance issues – the way that governance frameworks have been set up and modified over time and the how these mechanisms have functioned in practice. In Chapter 6 we look at the impact of transfer and its aftermath on housing management, and performance. Chapter 7 focuses on the financial profile and housing development activities of transfer HAs. An important factor here is the evolving relationship between a transfer landlord and its LA partner(s), an issue which is examined in more detail in Chapter 8. Finally, in Chapter 9 we pull together some of the main themes running through the research and discuss the policy implications for the future management of transfers and the landlords created through the process.

The stock transfer process

Introduction

This chapter looks at the factors that have motivated stock transfers and at the ways that these could impact on the shape and operation of the landlords created by the process. It then goes on to discuss how aspects of the national policy framework also have implications for the character of stock transfer HAs. Drawing mainly on case study evidence, it examines how local transfer processes and experiences can influence the structure and functioning of the landlords created as a result.

Motivations for transfer

LA stock disposals to other landlords have taken place over several decades. Until the end of the 1980s, however, these were mainly isolated experiments. Since then there has been a wave of stock transfers which, in time, may well lead to the end of council housing. This transfer wave was initially triggered by a number of policy and legislative developments in the 1980s. The Housing Acts of 1985 and 1988 were particularly important. The 1985 Act facilitated transfers as a 'voluntary' initiative by LAs where backed by tenants (hence the term 'Large-Scale Voluntary Transfer' – LSVT). This was originally intended as a means of bringing about the break up of council housing through partial transfers (Malpass and Mullins, 2002).

The 1988 Act, through its Tenants Choice provisions, was seen as presenting a threat to maintaining the integrity of LA housing services and this may have helped to prompt some transfers at this time as a means of 'protecting' the stock from 'predatory landlords'. Of much greater and more long-lasting significance, however, the Act effectively redefined HAs as non-public bodies. This freed associations from public sector borrowing constraints, thus providing a carrot for LAs seeking to escape from investment restrictions which limited their ability to maintain and improve their stock. To a greater or lesser extent, virtually all post-1988 stock transfers have been motivated by the scope for accessing investment resources through 'private finance' so as to redress repair and improvement backlogs.

For many English councils, the 1989 Local Government and Housing Act imposed further pressures by signalling often substantial rent increases to cross-subsidise local Housing Benefit expenditure from housing revenue accounts (HRAs). In many areas this was a powerful incentive for transfer into a HA regime where, until the end of the 1990s, there were no comparable controls on rents. Of equal or greater importance for some councils, the Act foreshadowed the restriction of councils' ability to recycle capital receipts into stock re-investment. In one of our case study areas, for example, the predecessor council's decision to transfer was strongly influenced by the prospect of a 35% rent increase simply to protect existing service levels, and by the need to cut its annual capital programme from £10 million to £3.5 million. Only by doubling rents could this capital funding gap have been filled.

Other factors contributing to the transfer impetus to a greater or lesser extent in different areas have included:

- a wish to 'protect' social housing from continued depletion through the Right to Buy (since this was not generally available to HA tenants);
- an aspiration to 'recycle' any transfer receipt into new social housing investment;
- an aspiration to use net transfer receipts (where generated) to invest in non-housing activities.

The prospect of operating in a less regulated and 'non-political' environment was also seen as attractive by some senior LA housing managers contemplating transfer in the late 1980s and early 1990s. In a similar vein, housing officers' enthusiasm for transfer has sometimes stemmed from a wish to end dependence on councils' direct labour organisations as repairs contractors.

As the 1990s progressed, some authorities came to see transfer as presenting a welcome opportunity to sidestep housing management compulsory competitive tendering (CCT) (Mullins et al, 1995). The prospect of local government reorganisation also helped to prompt some transfers. In one case study area, for example, an expectation that the shire district might be merged with neighbouring districts was seen as raising resource implications for the local housing service and this added to local transfer momentum.

Particularly since 1997, however, transfer as a means of accessing investment has become increasingly dominant as a motivating factor. Moves by central government to relieve residual housing debt (for example, through the Estate Regeneration Challenge Fund programme) have also helped to make the transfer option an attractive one for authorities for whom it was previously considered unfeasible.

While the utility of stock transfer has mainly been argued pragmatically in terms of facilitating investment and modernisation, it is fairly characterised as a 'politically driven policy' (Malpass and Mullins, 2002, p 684). Fundamentally, it could be argued, the policy is part of the 'modernisation project' that seeks to bring commercial disciplines to bear on the running of public services. An important consequence of this is to reduce the role of locally elected representatives in directly controlling such service provision.

The policy framework

From the outset, central government has, in principle, generally encouraged stock transfers. Partly through the requirement to obtain the Secretary of State's consent for transfers, the government can also influence the process and the shape of the organisations created through it. Of particular importance has been the insistence that transferring stock is passed into the ownership of registered HAs. Only for a short period in the early 1990s was this commitment in any doubt. This period saw the experimental creation of three transfer landlords (one in England, two in Scotland) in the shape of unregistered HAs with company-style boards incorporating senior staff and non-executive directors on equal terms. Partly to maximise the coverage of this research, one of these landlords is included among our 12 case study transfer HAs (see the Appendix).

In its first phase (1988-92) the stock transfer policy was largely driven in a bottom-up way by English LAs which saw housing handover as advantageous to their own circumstances. Only from 1993 did central government begin to impose greater control over the process in England by creating an annual transfer programme. The rules for aspiring transfer councils introduced under this regime included a size limit for individual transfers of 5,000 homes. More recently this has been increased to 12,000, a move justified by the assertion that "An RSL [Registered Social Landlord] with around 10,000 dwellings is regarded as achieving critical mass whereby it is of sufficient size to attract good quality staff and board members but small enough to be receptive and responsive to tenants' priorities" (DTLR, 2001, p 176). Councils wanting to transfer larger holdings were, therefore, required to split their stock across two or more successor landlords so that "one large monolithic landlord is not simply replaced by another" (DTLR, 2001, p 176).

The increasingly centrally directed nature of the policy in England was marked in 1997 by a government circular advising LAs that unreasonable resistance to transfer would incur financial penalties. In its 2000 Housing Green Paper (DETR, 2000), the Westminster administration reconfirmed a commitment to the policy by setting an annual transfer target of

200,000 homes as an essential component of its strategy for eliminating the disrepair backlog in council housing. Similarly, the Scottish Housing Green Paper (Scottish Office, 1999) had endorsed 'community ownership' as a vital means of channelling investment into the LA stock.

Nevertheless, while LAs in both England and Scotland have been pressed to consider transfer, the process has to be triggered at the local level and requires council ownership and commitment. The Scottish Homes transfer programme, by contrast, was an almost entirely top-down policy dictated by central government priorities. Alongside its regulatory role for HAs, the agency (set up in 1989) had inherited the stock of some 75,000 homes accumulated by the former Scottish Special HA. The transfer of this stock into the ownership of locally based HAs was a fundamental corporate objective set for Scottish Homes by central government at the outset. While local interests were able to influence the nature of Scottish Homes transfers, there was no opportunity to consider the policy's appropriateness in local circumstances, nor to 'opt out' of its implementation.

Registration criteria

In terms of shaping the new landlords created through stock transfer, central government influence is mainly transmitted through the registration and regulatory requirements operated by The Housing Corporation and Communities Scotland (which replaced Scottish Homes in 2001). While newly established transfer HAs have always needed to meet the regulator's standard expectations for registration, guidance specific to this context has been produced by the Corporation since 1996. Of particular importance here are the regulations on the make-up of a transfer association's governing board. Until 1996 the rules limited LA representation on a governing board to 20%. At the same time, the rules as they applied in England disallowed combined tenant and council representation exceeding 49% (Wilcox et al, 1993).

Since 1996, equal board member representation for council nominees, tenants and 'independents' has been allowed in both England and Scotland under the so-called 'local housing company' model. However, since most north of the border transfer HAs have been established through

transfers of Scottish Homes (rather than LA) stock, councillor representation on the boards of these bodies has generally been small-scale (see Chapter 5). Tenant-controlled HAs have, on the other hand, been a familiar form of social landlord for some time in Scotland and Scottish Homes, as HA regulator, pursued an explicit policy of encouraging the development of tenant-controlled transfer landlords.

However, while HA board members may be appointed by virtue of their 'constituency background', it should be borne in mind that, as emphasised by regulatory guidance, they are expected to operate as individuals and not as 'representatives' in the strict sense. For example, Housing Corporation guidance for prospective board members emphasises that they "have a primary responsibility to the new RSL and its future success, irrespective of the constituency that has led to (their) appointment.... The board needs to develop a close working relationship and work together corporately without factions" (Housing Corporation, 1998a, p 7)[2].

Another aspect of registration rules that can impact significantly on the nature of transfer HAs relates to staff recruitment. While Transfer of Undertakings Protection of Employment (TUPE) regulations confer certain obligations as regards a LA's existing workforce, The Housing Corporation has become increasingly insistent that newly established HAs should openly advertise senior posts (Housing Corporation, 1998b). By reducing the likelihood that the new landlord will be run by the former LA's housing management team, this might increase the chances of the new body seeing itself as wholly independent of its 'parent council'.

This emphasis on the need for transfer HAs to operate independently is at the heart of the registration rules as they relate to this class of landlord (Housing Corporation, 1998a). So as to establish a clear and separate identity, new landlords are, for example, required to move to their own offices within a year of set-up.

In practice, newly established (whole stock) transfer associations tend to have taken on most of their staff from the predecessor landlord. This has usually included senior staff, so that in the

---

[2] With this in mind, 'representatives' is put in inverted commas in this report.

case of LA transfers the former director of housing has typically become the new chief executive. The typical approach employed among early LA transfers in England was to open up vacancies to 'external' candidates only if there was no 'natural candidate' from within the existing housing department staff (Mullins et al, 1992). More recently, according to the National Housing Federation, there has been a greater tendency for senior staff – particularly finance directors – to be recruited from outside the transferring council. Nevertheless, most new landlords are, generally, initially staffed by the same people who performed a similar function under the predecessor landlord.

Changes in the funding regime

Another significant national policy change introduced at about the same time as the local housing company model was the possibility of public funding to facilitate transfers of 'negative value' stock – that is, where the cost of outstanding repairs exceeded the gross valuation. For many LAs and for individual estates, this opened up a previously impossible transfer option. A key channel for this 'debt relief' was the Estate Regeneration Challenge Fund (ERCF) programme as operated from 1996-99. ERCF was crucial in giving rise to most of the English 'partial transfers' as enumerated in Table 2. This programme was notable in facilitating the creation of a cohort of new local housing company-style associations, mainly established as

subsidiaries of large existing associations (see Chapter 3).

Particularly in England, successive changes in the national policy regime mean that a transfer association's era of establishment is likely to have a long-lasting impact on its character. Partly for this reason, national stakeholder organisations see a distinct threefold categorisation of English transfer HAs, as shown in Table 4.

Local transfer processes and their legacy

Most transfer proposals involve a set of precise commitments to tenants to make good backlogs of disrepair, to undertake specified improvements within a finite period (typically five years), and to maintain rents at specified levels during this time. In England, these repairs and improvements have been geared increasingly to achieving the government's 'decent homes' target. But throughout the history of LSVTs, tenants have had the right to a ballot on the proposed transfer, and experience has shown that majority tenants' consent for landlord proposals cannot be taken for granted.

Where transfer is seriously contested, there can be a legacy with long-lasting effects. This can be reflected in post-transfer relationships between the transfer landlord and its LA counterpart, and between the association and tenants 'representatives'. It can also result in tension and conflict at board level, in some cases associated

Table 4: Broad typology of English transfer associations

Group	Era of establishment	Area type	Stock condition/ financial position	Funding	Organisation type	Constitution
I	Mainly pre-freestanding agency	Rural 1997 majority	Good condition stock, districts	Private net positive value	Newly created	'Independent' finance
II	Mainly 1996-99	Inner cities	Poor condition stock, negative value	ERCF[a], private finance	Existing HA or newly created subsidiary of (larger) existing HA	Local Housing Company model
III	Post-1997	Urban areas	Largely poor condition stock, negative value	Debt relief, private finance	Newly created HA	Local Housing Company model

[a] ERCF = Estate Regeneration Challenge Fund.
Source: Based on National Housing Federation typology

with attempts to incorporate 'transfer sceptics' as tenant board members (see Chapter 4).

Post-transfer relations between the council and transfer HA can also be prejudiced by the sometimes acrimonious negotiation in advance of the transaction. As observed in another recent study, such negotiations can lead to "a souring of relationships among former colleagues … resentments can linger, which tend to affect their ongoing working relationships" (Taper et al, 2003, para 3.120).

For housing staff, the transfer process often serves as a catalyst for engagement with tenants on an unprecedented scale. The boost to tenant activism may lead to the development of post-transfer participation structures far more sophisticated than those which previously existed (although the impetus for actual engagement is liable to be quite short-lived once the post-transfer 'hump' of repair and improvement work is complete). For many staff, too, the inherently forward-looking nature of the process, together with the intense working atmosphere generated by the need to draw up new plans and structures inside tight deadlines, generates a new sense of shared purpose. This can strengthen working relationships and underpin a strong sense of cohesiveness among transferring staff.

Decisions taken during the immediate pre-transfer period on key business plan components – for example on stock valuation, rent guarantees, interpretation of stock condition data – have a long-lasting legacy which influence (and sometimes constrain) the longer-term evolution of the organisation. Sometimes these are significantly affected by the experience of the transfer process itself. In one case study area, for example, an appreciation of organised opposition to transfer led to the council adding a number of 'golden conditions' to the transfer agreement. These conditions, incorporated in the agreement as covenants, responded specifically to concerns voiced by transfer opponents. For example, the new landlord was bound to:

- undertake the upgrading of pre-reinforced concrete (PRC) homes within 15 years 'to a mortgageable standard';
- employ the same number of sheltered housing wardens (as pre-transfer) subject to adequate continuing demand.

In practice, these obligations have been found to impose significant constraints on the new landlord and are argued to be inimical to tenants' collective interests. For example, the undertaking on PRC homes commits the association to heavy investment, some of it relating to houses which, under an economically rational strategy, would be better refurbished to a lower standard or demolished and replaced with modern housing (possibly at higher densities). For some of the houses concerned, refurbishment 'to a mortgageable standard' is seen as being a technical impossibility. For others the investment could be seen as economically unwise in that the homes could be subsequently bought under the Right to Buy (RTB) at a fraction of the cost committed to their refurbishment. In addition, post-transfer survey evidence suggests that some PRC homes are perfectly sound and not in need of major refurbishment.

It is interesting to note that The Housing Corporation saw no reason for withholding registration from the association encumbered with these obligations. The Corporation's general position on such matters is that associations and LAs need to be able to negotiate reasonably if 'transfer commitments' prove unrealistic in practice. Transfer contracts are therefore expected to incorporate mechanisms to facilitate flexibility in implementing such commitments where unforeseen circumstances may impede this.

In another case study, pressures encouraging the raising of potentially unfulfillable expectations resulted more from a 'beauty contest' between contending transfer landlords than from a need to maximise tenant support for the transfer proposal itself. Ideas for regenerating a retail centre alongside housing refurbishment were seen as crucial in having swung tenant support behind the successful HA rather than its competitors. However, these plans were never formally included in the transfer agreement and it subsequently became clear that no provision was ever made for the funding of the works involved. While they were not incorporated among the new landlord's 'transfer promises' as such, the association's inability to implement these ideas prejudiced post-transfer relations with residents and other local interests.

In a third case study, an early 1990s transfer, the council's transfer plans included the setting up of a decentralised network of local offices, replacing what had been a fairly centralised style of operation. While these proposals were not borne of any particular concern about the lack of adequate tenant backing for transfer, it was believed that, as demonstrable 'service improvements', they would help to bolster tenant support. Within a few years, however, the transfer landlord had come to the view that its area-based approach was a costly irrelevance, its maintenance being somewhat symbolic since workload monitoring showed that some offices, at least, were operating at well below capacity. Because of the association's need to generate revenue savings, it then planned to re-centralise its operations. Unfortunately, because of the original presentation of the area offices as fundamental to service improvement post-transfer, this provoked substantial tenant disquiet and was difficult to achieve.

The formal decisions facilitating any stock transfer are made by council members, central government, the regulator and eligible tenants. As Gardiner et al (1991) argued, however, a number of other stakeholder groups are also involved in the process. A theme running through many of our case studies is the council officer-driven nature of the process. Although LA members occasionally play a leading role in pushing a transfer forward, the more common scenario is where their endorsement is obtained only through substantial lobbying on the part of senior housing department staff. While anti-transfer campaigners are inclined to portray such enthusiasm as little more than self-interest, this is simplistic. In our view, it stems at least in part from a wish to operate a more professional service. This has significant implications for the development and operation of the landlords created through the transfer process.

3

Organisational structures

Introduction

Drawing on postal survey and case study evidence, as well as regulatory data, this chapter looks at the organisational structures established by transfer HAs and at the way these have developed over time. Following a brief review of existing research evidence, it discusses the extent to which the initial structure of transfer HAs resembles that of former landlords and the influences which shape these configurations. We examine whether transfer creates flatter, less hierarchical structures and whether, in their subsequent evolution, transfer HAs are becoming more or less generic in their form and operation. Lastly, we focus on the restructuring of transfer HAs involving participation in group structures.

Previous research evidence

There is broad agreement that considerable organisational restructuring has been taking place throughout the HA sector in recent years (Pollitt et al, 1998; Walker, 1998, 2000; Mullins et al, 2001). Walker (1998) identifies a major driver of change as being HAs' relationship with and reliance on private finance institutions. This can be attributed to the 1988 Housing Act which marked the effective start of the mixed public/ private finance regime. The consequent 'exposure to risk' was seen by Walker as having taken associations 'from comfort to competition'. As a result, it is argued, 'efficiency drives' remain dominant within the sector, underpinning many of the pressures affecting associations – including the impression that organisations are moving away from their traditional 'welfare' role and towards a more property-centred approach.

Most recent studies of organisational restructuring within the HA sector have drawn on the New Public Management (NPM) literature, for example Pollitt et al (1998), Walker (1998, 2000, 2001) and Mullins et al (2001). Those working within this framework have categorised the structural and managerial changes occurring in associations within broad trends seen to be taking place across the public sector more broadly. Such trends include administrative decentralisation (Pollitt et al, 1998), 'decentralisation', 'downsizing' and 'efficiency drives' (Walker, 1998), and externalisation and managerialisation (Walker, 2000, 2001).

Although there has been little or no specific research on the way that transfer landlords evolve over time, earlier studies have documented the immediate impact of transfer on housing service structures and cultures. For example, while LA whole stock and Scottish Homes transfers have typically involved newly created landlord bodies taking on the staff of the former landlord, Mullins et al (1995) found that considerable organisational and cultural change typically arose from transfer. This included adjustments to meet the requirements of funders and regulators, the establishment of novel internal management and decision-making structures, and the negotiation of new relationships with tenants.

Broadly consistent findings were reported by Pollitt et al (1998), who found significant changes in organisational culture post-transfer. New associations created to take on transferred stock were seen as having changed "to some extent towards the HA culture, but had also changed that culture, being seen as unusually aggressive within the movement" (p 144). Transfer HAs' organisational innovations reported in the Pollitt et al study included the adoption of customer care strategies and performance related-pay schemes. On the other hand, as the authors conceded, some changes of this kind might have happened in the absence of transfer in that similar developments were taking place among LA landlords during the period concerned.

Similarly, evidence from a study by Mullins and Riseborough (2000) identified changes in managerial and staffing structures taking place across the HA sector, with leaders striving to promote organisational restructuring while retaining a degree of internal stability. In another study which looked at the HA sector as a whole, Scott et al (2001) found that there was a lack of organisational stability within HAs, with "half of the [Scottish] associations surveyed [indicating] that some form of re-organisation had taken place" recently (p 23).

Fresh evidence

Organisational innovation?

Partly in order to secure the support of council members and tenants, stock transfer is often presented as solely a means of accessing investment resources: a technical evasion of public sector borrowing requirement restrictions. Portraying transfer as a 'minimum change' option in terms of service structure and delivery has been seen as a key means of securing local endorsement (Mullins et al, 1992). Such a scenario has prompted some critics (for example Robertson, 2003) to suggest that transfer can amount to little more than a financial ruse where 'housing association' is substituted for 'council' on the office nameplate.

Sometimes the stress on 'minimum change' runs deeper than a campaigning tactic and reflects a belief that 'highly performing' structures should be preserved as far as possible. Given the pre-transfer housing department's consistent record as a 'top performer,' as recorded by housing management performance indicators, this was seen as a crucial consideration in Sunderland Council's 2001 transfer to Sunderland Housing Group. In a recent transfer by another northern authority, exactly the opposite view was taken: the transfer being seen as a welcome opportunity

to restructure so as to promote cultural renewal of an under-performing housing service.

In practice, however, our case study evidence suggests that the structure of newly created transfer HAs typically differs substantially from that of the predecessor landlord. Not all LAs have traditionally operated housing as a distinct service which could, in any event, be simply re-badged, en bloc. In smaller district councils, in particular, housing services have often been structured in a fairly disparate way. And even in the most 'comprehensive' of housing departments, services such as finance and legal support are typically provided to housing managers by other departments. Incorporating staff performing these functions within a newly created HA inevitably creates a structure different from that of the pre-transfer regime.

The structural novelty of newly created HAs was apparent in many case studies. In one instance, for example, the predecessor LA regime had involved staff with a housing role being split across 16 former council divisions. From the perspective of many staff, moreover, the creation of a single-purpose body in place of a loosely linked constellation of former LA departments is one of the main attractions and benefits of transfer and helps to underpin greater professionalism, improved managerial performance and employee satisfaction.

For many newly created HAs, an initial stress on the need to build or acquire a new headquarters office is motivated partly by the aspiration to unite previously scattered staff as a means of developing – and securing staff loyalty to – a distinct corporate identity. The fact that available and affordable sites or buildings tend to be located in urban fringe locations less accessible to tenants, however, means that such moves have some potentially negative implications.

Through its imposition of a maximum size limit, central government rules have also been intended to ensure substantial structural change where a council with more than the threshold number (currently 12,000, although about to be relaxed) wishes to undertake a whole stock transfer. Nevertheless, it could be argued that 'group and satellite' transfers structured to accommodate these rules may, in any case, have allowed the reproduction of a housing department plus district office model under a different guise.

In some respects, the experience of LA partial transfers and of ex-Scottish Homes transfers has been distinct from that described above. In the former, scope for organisational innovation has often been enhanced by the fact that former landlord staff seem less likely to be taken on by the new landlord. Where a council retains a substantial landlord function, it retains scope to redeploy staff formerly involved in managing a transferred estate or neighbourhood. In both our case studies involving partial transfer HAs, the new landlord's workforce had been entirely externally recruited. At the same time, the status of many such organisations as group subsidiaries means that there are questions about their degree of independence. In both these case studies, for example, the chief officer's title of 'director' (rather than chief executive) appeared to signify their role as effectively that of district manager within a larger structure.

Scottish Homes transfers, by contrast, seem to have been more liable to be regarded as a 'management buy-out' whereby a new organisation – complete with existing staff – is largely carved out of an existing area office structure. That said, such examples share with all other transfer landlords the incorporation of 'corporate' functions such as finance, personnel and IT within a unified, single-purpose organisation.

Aside from the need to accommodate 'Transfer of Undertakings: Protection of Employment' (TUPE) requirements, to externally advertise senior posts and to avoid 'unnecessary' change at transfer,

what other factors affect decisions on how to structure the new landlord body? As earlier research has observed, a key role here is often played by consultants: "Local authorities, tenants and prospective landlords [have] often found that choices about organisational form and accountability arrangements were limited by what was on offer from established advisers rather than what was possible under legislation and regulation" (Malpass and Mullins, 2002, p 680). Consultants' models, therefore, have tended to produce a degree of standardisation.

More commonly, LAs influence transfer landlords' organisational structures through their decisions on which non-landlord housing functions to retain under their direct control. In particular, the day-to-day operation of homelessness assessment and housing register management may (under the English framework) be out-sourced by LAs. While such contracts can be (and occasionally are) made with bodies other than the local transfer landlord, the vast majority of councils out-sourcing these services contract them to their transfer HA counterparts (see Table 5). About half of all English whole stock transfer landlords, therefore, operate housing register management and/or homelessness assessment on behalf of their 'parent council'. The ways that these functions are incorporated within the organisation usually reflects the pre-existing LA structure. For the most part, therefore, they are operated as discrete centralised units. The broader significance of LA–transfer HA client–contractor relationships of this kind is discussed in Chapter 8.

Table 5: Whole stock transfer LAs/LSVT associations in England: combination of contracted–out functions relating to the management of access to social housing

Agency responsible for housing register management	Agency responsible for assessment of homelessness applications		
	LA % of all transfer LAs	LSVT HA % of all transfer LAs	Total % of all transfer LAs
LA	49	2	51
LSVT HA	18	31	49
Total	67	33	100

Note: Table excludes the authority where the relevant functions are contracted out to a third party HA.
Source: Pawson and Mullins (2003), based on postal survey November/December 2001

Hierarchy

Freed from the hierarchical traditions of local government, transfer HAs tend to adopt flatter, leaner structures. While postal survey evidence suggests that such changes are far from universal (see Table 5), it should be borne in mind that most, if not all, newly created HAs take on a wider range of functions than were previously managed by the LA director of housing (see above). There is, therefore, a clear logic to the creation of a chief executive post above that of the 'LA director of housing equivalent' in a new HA. Bearing this in mind, it is notable that in 71% of instances, the number of tiers of management in English whole stock transfer HAs is the same or less than in their predecessor council (see Table 6).

Flatter structures have tended to be favoured as in keeping with a wish to empower staff and devolve managerial responsibility to a greater degree than has been typical of LA landlords. (Implications for organisational culture are discussed in Chapter 4.) The great majority of postal survey respondents (97% of responding English HAs) believed that the changes to the staffing structure of their organisation compared with the predecessor LA involved greater delegation of responsibility towards middle managers and staff. A substantial majority (68% of respondents) also believed that the restructuring of their organisation was dissimilar from the kinds of changes being experienced by landlord LAs.

Post-transfer restructuring

Since the staffing structure established in the immediate aftermath of transfer, most new landlords have reconfigured their staffing arrangements. This applies to 80% of English transfer associations and 60% of their Scottish counterparts. In general, the likelihood of staffing reorganisation is related to the length of time an organisation has been in existence. For example, only 17% of 1988-96 landlords retained the structures inherited immediately following transfer, while among associations set up more recently, the comparable figure was 30%. A majority of the longer-established English landlords have restructured themselves two or more times since set-up.

The main features of staffing structure reorganisation frequently mentioned in postal survey responses included the creation of flatter structures and the need to move away from a generic management style and towards a more functionally specialised operating style.

Frequently, budgetary pressures resulting from unforeseen circumstances (for example, the introduction of a rent restructuring regime) have prompted recently set-up HAs to review and reshape their employee structure. Sometimes this is anticipated in the business plan: it is recognised before transfer that, in its initial shape, the new organisation will have to carry forward certain 'excess costs' perhaps owing to a need to accommodate LA sensibilities in advance of transfer. Notional staff cost savings are therefore factored into the plan from, say, Year 3. In at least two case studies, for example, major reorganisations after two to three years were mainly designed to eliminate costs associated with obligations of this kind. In any case, the speed with which transfers need to be pushed through after ballot endorsement leaves precious little time to carry out any thorough review of staffing requirements below senior management level. Such reviews must, of necessity, wait until the new regime has bedded down. By this time,

Table 6: Whole stock transfer landlords in England: staffing structure as compared with predecessor LA housing department (%)

Current number of tiers of management in relation to predecessor LA	Era of establishment		
	1988–96	1997–99	All
More than LA	26	36	29
Same as LA	26	27	26
Less than LA	48	36	45
Total	100	100	100
Number of respondents	27	11	38

the new landlord has often accumulated sufficient unfilled vacancies to permit any required slimming down without the need for compulsory job losses.

Many other factors may trigger the need for the reorganisation of staffing. Examples cited by the case study HAs include the need to 'make best use of existing skills' or to 'respond to increasing complexity of service provision'. In one case study association a major remodelling of the staffing structure arose from the chief executive's view that the organisation had become excessively opportunistic and development-led. Reflecting a perception that development needed to be better integrated with management, this function was decentralised to area (management) teams. Concurrently, the senior management team was reduced from five to three by creating an operations director to oversee both development and management activities.

Structural evolution: genericism versus functional specialisation

How does transfer affect the balance between generic and specialist roles in the housing service? The vast majority of English transfer HAs believe that 'regime change' has an impact here – only six of the 44 postal survey respondents judged that there had been 'little change' in the balance between genericism and specialisation post-transfer. However, the evidence is unclear as to the overall direction of change (see Table 7).

Case study evidence helps to explain this apparent conundrum: it probably reflects the difference between the immediate and longer-term impact of transfer. A common scenario has involved initial post-transfer moves towards a more generic structure and style of operation, with these changes being subsequently rolled back. Overall, therefore, longer-term evolution is tending towards increased functional specialisation and centralisation.

These moves often revolve around decisions to adopt more specialist approaches to rent collection and arrears management. This could reflect the nature of transfer HAs as independent landlords with an overriding need to meet business plan income assumptions and targets. Indeed, a clear majority (67%) of postal survey respondents believed that such changes were a specific response to the landlord's new institutional status, while few (23%) accepted the proposition that they were little different from developments taking place contemporaneously in landlord LAs. Implicit here is the view that rent collection is typically given insufficient priority under generic regimes.

Group structures

While very few whole stock transfer HAs have been set up as group subsidiaries, most have subsequently examined or developed group arrangements (see below). Such developments, where enacted, are often the most fundamental aspects of post-transfer organisational restructuring. While such a trend is undoubtedly common across the HA sector as a whole, it has distinct implications for transfer landlords.

A group structure is "a formal association of separate organisations" (Audit Commission and Housing Corporation, 2001, p 3). Across the sector as a whole, such arrangements have become increasingly common in recent years (in England, at least). This has occurred for a variety of reasons, including the perceived need to respond to:

- aspects of the regulatory regime;
- changes to the tax system;
- opportunities to diversify – both functionally and geographically;

Table 7: Post-transfer tendencies towards genericism or functional specialisation (number of responding HAs)

Jurisdiction	Staff roles generally more generic?		Staff roles generally more specialised?	
	Agree	Disagree	Agree	Disagree
England	23	11	22	13
Scotland	10	4	5	8

- the need to organise existing functional and/ or geographically diverse activities (Audit Commission and Housing Corporation, 2001, p 4).

Postal survey evidence shows that among the majority of English transfer landlords set up as freestanding organisations, almost all (90%) had subsequently considered setting up or joining a group structure. A third had also considered the merger option. Deliberations on these possibilities have been somewhat less common among Scottish transfer landlords: five of the 15 Scottish respondents reported having looked at the possibility of becoming involved in a group structure, while two others had examined the merger option.

In many cases, post-set-up consideration of the group structure option by English transfer landlords has led to subsequent moves in this direction. The result is that, of those covered in our survey, exactly half reported having set up or joined group structures. Six of the 23 organisations involved (26%) had also merged with others to form a new group. Two landlords had opted for post-set-up mergers rather than group structures. Housing Corporation registration data confirms that 60% of all English transfer landlords in existence in 2001 (including those set up since 1999) were party to group structures, with 39% being technically subsidiaries of other organisations (see Table 8).

In most cases the organisations to which transfer landlords relate as subsidiaries are also HAs themselves – for the most part, of the 'conventional' variety. Forty per cent of subsidiary transfer landlords, however, relate to 'superior' bodies which are not stock-owning HAs themselves. In most cases these are likely to

be 'holding companies' set up as a 'group centre' for two or more subsidiary associations.

In Scotland the picture is rather different. Only just over a quarter of transfer landlords (27%) had set up or joined groups by 2001, according to Communities Scotland regulatory data (unpublished). Transfer landlords were slightly less likely than their 'conventional' HA counterparts to have entered group structure arrangements (36% of non-transfer HAs were party to group structures in 2001). Whether this comparison holds true in the English context is, however, unknown.

Among English transfer landlords set up within, or subsequently joining, group structures, the commonest 'main reasons' for having done so were:

- to facilitate economies of scale (26%);
- to benefit from the financial strength of a partner organisation (22%);
- to derive borrowing advantages (17%);
- to facilitate geographical expansion (17%).

According to postal survey responses, the vast majority of English landlords remaining freestanding at the time of the survey (87%), anticipated joining (or forming) a group structure within the next five years. Even in Scotland a third of respondents not currently in group structures anticipated joining or establishing a group within this timeframe.

Case study evidence suggests that a clear distinction needs to be made between 'external collaboration' (or 'type 1') group structures which involve an association mainly intending to facilitate expansion through partnership with another landlord and those which involve the setting up of non-landlord subsidiaries ('internal

Table 8: Group structure relationships of English transfer landlords (2001) (%)

Organisational status	Partial	Whole stock	All
Is subsidiary only	64	24	30
Is subsidiary and has one or more subsidiaries	0	11	9
Has one or more subsidiaries only	18	21	20
Freestanding	18	44	40
Total	100	100	100
Number of organisations	22	106	128

Source: Housing Corporation registration data (unpublished)

group' or 'type 2' group structures). These latter initiatives sometimes involve detaching elements from an HA's existing structure (for example the works department). Type 1 group proposals are often motivated by an aspiration to generate economies of scale through the creation of shared corporate functions. Although they may involve a degree of functional integration, the essential feature of such a 'group' is that – as distinct from a full-scale merger – the parties retain a degree of separateness and independence. Type 2 group structures, by contrast, tend to reflect a desire for functional diversification.

Given the established LA preference for transferring stock to newly created rather than existing HAs (see Table 3), a transfer HA's post-set-up move to form a type 1 group is clearly liable to generate tensions. In one of our case study HAs, for example, moves to set up such arrangements in the mid-1990s had caused conflict with the former LA and contributed to the resignation of the then chief executive who was identified with the plans. Under the proposals, a group centre organisation would have been set up, with the existing association becoming a subsidiary of that body. Crucially, however, the plans envisaged the ownership of transferred stock from the existing association to the new body. The purpose of this 'cross-collateralisation' was to facilitate group expansion through taking on further stock transfer landlords as subsidiary agencies. Pooling ownership in the group centre would, it was argued, facilitate borrowing against asset values at favourable rates. The case study HA's parent council, however, saw this as 'using the council's silver for the benefit of other areas' and its determined opposition helped to sink the plan.

In another case study, a group structure proposal involving collaboration with another large association had caused substantial dissension at board level. Faced with majority opposition to the plan, the then board chair and a number of allies resigned their seats.

Staff, too, may be unenthusiastic about relinquishing the self-contained organisational independence often seen as a major advantage over working in a LA environment where housing is often a relatively small player with very limited autonomy. Plans for group

structures of this kind often need to strike a difficult balance between retaining a measure of independence alongside sufficient integration to make such moves financially viable and worthwhile. Such dilemmas will be faced by any HA; for transfer landlords, however, their origins, their LA parentage and their governance arrangements (see Chapter 5) are likely to make them all the sharper.

The experience of another case study HA in setting up a type 1 group structure is instructive in the light it sheds on the motivations and processes involved. Within a few years of its establishment in 1991, the association concerned – Suffolk Heritage HA (SHHA) – had developed an aspiration for partnership with another HA. In 1998, the association came together with Peddars Way HA (PWHA), another transfer landlord based some 50 miles distant. Together, the partners formed the Flagship Group. The constituent parts of Flagship remain legally distinct group members, and for the purposes of communication with tenants, SHHA and PWHA remain very much alive. However, the collaboration is commonly referred to by staff as 'the merger' because central services from PWHA and SHHA were merged. The managerial preference for the term 'group member' rather than 'subsidiary' is emblematic of a concern to avoid 'downgrading' of PWHA and SHHA as definable entities.

The main objectives of setting up the group were:

- to achieve revenue savings through economies of scale by sharing the costs of corporate functions;
- to open up the possibility of revenue savings through rationalising property management, given the geographical overlap of SHHA and PWHA stock;
- to derive borrowing advantages from the ability to secure loans against a larger stock (cross-collateralisation).

Since its creation, the Flagship collaboration has involved an increasingly integrated approach across the two main group member HAs. Under its latest 'whole group approach' phase, recently enacted, Flagship now employs the top two tiers of staff, as well as those carrying out corporate, group-wide functions. Neither SHHA nor PWHA retains its own chief executive, for example.

The revenue savings created through the partial merging of functions within Flagship have been substantial, equating to £4 per week per tenant. This needs to be seen in the context of recent research suggesting that HA group structures set up with the primary motivation of achieving financial savings are rarely successful in this respect (Audit Commission and Housing Corporation, 2002, p 33). This may well reflect the political difficulties of achieving the balancing of functional integration and group subsidiary autonomy and identity.

Four other case study associations had set up, or were planning to establish, type 2 group structures – that is, 'floating off' existing elements of the organisation to form semi-autonomous subsidiaries. Such 'internal group' arrangements were seen as facilitating the organisations' involvement in 'diverse activities' – that is, activities distinct from an association's 'core business' in the development and management of social housing. Examples cited by case study HAs included the development of market rented housing. Arrangements of this kind were also seen as potentially beneficial in limiting Corporation Tax liabilities as well as in providing a greater sense of identity for different parts of the business. This might possibly help to encourage group subsidiary leaders to strive for better performance. In addition, it could help facilitate greater entrepreneurialism among these leaders, for example, in relation to selling services to other organisations.

Group structures have a different connotation in the context of transfer HAs set up as subsidiaries of existing associations. Three of our case studies (one whole stock transfer and two partial transfer HAs) were of this type. Arrangements of this sort are, for several reasons, commonplace in the partial transfer context. First, the frequently challenging nature of partial transfer schemes, where physical and social problems are often deeply ingrained, is seen as calling for a well-established and experienced operator (while, at the same time, providing at least a semblance of 'local control'). Second, the financial reserves a large, well-established association may be willing to apply are seen as important in the context of typically heavy investment needs. And, third, a group parent association may be able to help by offering is own 'unencumbered' stock as a security against private financing of the scheme.

Reflecting the wider trend in favour of mergers across the sector as a whole, the evidence from 'transfer HA as subsidiary' case studies seems to suggest an ongoing tendency towards functional integration between parent bodies and subsidiaries. Such moves, generally presented as efficiency measures required to meet business plan targets, tend to make subsidiaries more dependent on and less autonomous from their parent associations. This can lead to tensions with predecessor LAs which had originally envisaged creating local housing companies over which they (rather than parent HAs) would retain significant influence. Transfer HA staff, too, may see such moves as betraying pre-ballot promises of local autonomy. The often acute nature of such tensions may help to explain what appears to be a relatively high level of turnover among subsidiary HA chief officers.

4

Staff management and organisational culture

Organisational culture and its significance

The managerial structures adopted by transfer HAs were discussed in Chapter 3. These arrangements have implications for the organisational cultures of the new landlords. Organisational culture is a difficult concept to pin down but can be summarised as 'how things are done round here' (Holder et al, 1998). While the usual publicly stated case for transfer rests mainly on its capacity for opening up access to capital investment (see Chapter 2), the policy is also significantly motivated by a belief that it can lead to "a substantive [and beneficial] change of culture in the management of ... housing" (DETR, 2000, p 63). In particular, it is hoped that transfer will stimulate a more 'consumerist' style of housing management as well as bringing gains in more 'bread and butter' efficiency and effectiveness terms. These, in turn, are likely to be achievable only through empowering and engaging staff in ways that mark a distinct shift in organisational culture.

The importance of changing organisational culture in securing improved service delivery has been emphasised by Hartley and Rashman (2002). They noted "many positive changes in organisational design" (p 8) in transfer HAs, including:

- an increased focus on customer service;
- increased partnering;
- human resources strategies;
- a strong emphasis on training and development;
- performance-related pay;
- flatter (less hierarchical) structures.

Drawing mainly on case study evidence, this chapter looks at the staff management practices of transfer landlords and the organisational cultures with which these are closely associated. Again, we are interested both in the comparison between new landlords and their predecessor bodies, and in the way that these successor agencies have been developing over time.

Earlier studies have shown that transfer can lead to a clear boost in staff morale, perhaps attributable to closer identification with the association (Pollitt et al, 1998), greater responsibilities and career opportunities (Graham, 1997) and a more general sense of empowerment (Taylor, 2000). It is, of course, possible that heavy-handed attempts to impose a new management culture could seriously undermine organisational morale although evidence from our own case studies suggests that such scenarios are relatively unusual in the transfer context. Generally, the impact of transfer on staff and staff morale has been attributed to a number of factors, including how the transfer process was managed, especially where the process was long drawn out and there was a lack of appropriate training (Graham, 1997).

Impact of initial recruitment

Since most staff taken on by newly established transfer HAs are former employees of the predecessor landlord, the creation of a transformed landlord culture is likely to be something of a challenge. As case study evidence confirms, however, most new landlords recruit some staff externally, and these individuals can make an important contribution to introducing a new style of operation from that of the agency's 'parent body'. Among senior management team appointments, finance directors, in particular, are commonly recruited from outwith the predecessor landlord. In the process of helping the association to develop a new identity and culture, these recruits often play the role of a 'necessary irritant' (Rochester and Hutchison, 2002).

Over time, of course, the influence of predecessor landlords transmitted through transferred staff begins to wane, as employee turnover gradually reduces their numbers. In 2002, for example, one case study HA retained only 10 of the original 98 former housing department staff taken on at set up in 1990. Many of their successors are recruited from within the HA sector, and this is seen as contributing to a cultural shift towards sector-wide norms (although these norms, themselves, are gradually shifting as a result of transfer landlords' growing presence).

Balance between business and social imperatives

HAs are independent bodies exposed to financial risk. Such risks are particularly relevant to transfer bodies, given their debt-funded status. "Whilst all RSLs need to be businesslike in the way they go about their work, transfer organisations are quite explicitly set up as businesses...." (Rochester and Hutchison, 2002). Transfer HAs' exposure to risk might be expected to produce a different balance between business and social objectives from that prevailing in a LA (or other state housing organisation) where formal bankruptcy is not seen as a possibility. The views of senior staff in most transfer associations are consistent with this.

Only two of the 61 respondents in our postal survey believed that the balance between 'business' and 'social' objectives was 'no different in their organisation from what it had been within the predecessor landlord' (LA or Scottish Homes). Likewise, only two transfer bodies considered that their organisation's balance between business and social objectives had changed in ways similar to those common in LA housing departments. The prevailing view, then, is consistent with Walker's (1998) argument that HAs have moved further than most public sector

organisations in the direction of New Public Management (NPM) approaches (see Chapter 3).

Case study evidence confirms that, by comparison with predecessor organisations, a greatly increased staff sensitivity to corporate objectives and targets tends to permeate transfer landlords throughout the staff hierarchy. To some extent, this just reflects what was, at least until recently, the 'alien' nature of key concepts and terminology in the LA sector: "I had never heard the term 'business plan' when we were part of the council" (middle manager in a 1999 transfer association). It was, nevertheless, striking that even among front-line staff, awareness of the importance attached to association's business plans was generally widespread. This often seemed to have encouraged strategic, longer-term thinking throughout the organisation, as well as laying foundations essential for the development of a performance culture.

Related to staff 'ownership' of transfer HA corporate objectives is the observation of one case study interviewee that the transfer had helped to displace the 'blame culture' seen as prevalent under the previous council regime. Rather than seeking to pin responsibility for problems on others – councillors, government spending cuts, and so on – staff were now more inclined to accept responsibility for things going wrong and to see it as their job to sort them out.

Given transfer landlord staff members' grasp of business plan imperatives, an awareness of their organisation's overall financial position is often quite well formed, even at lower levels of the hierarchy. This fact is clearly exemplified by the recent finding from parallel research that "[transfer HA] staff have an unusually high degree of understanding of their employer's objectives, which 69 per cent of staff at all levels say they understand (this is 31 percentage points higher than the LA norm and 16 per cent higher than for the public sector (as a whole)" (Taper et al, 2003, para 3.11). In particular, the high – and rising – level of indebtedness which characterises most transfer associations' early years is generally well appreciated throughout the organisation and can leave a lasting impact on attitudes. Among some longer-established associations, for example, this is seen as having underpinned the development of a 'thrift culture' which may prove difficult to eradicate once peak debt is passed and surpluses begin to be generated (see Chapter 6).

Staff empowerment

A substantial degree of 'ownership' of organisational objectives is often fostered by transfer HAs through the creation of flatter managerial structures and the associated greater delegation of responsibility (see Chapter 3). Other staff management practices that typically contribute include the practice of staff 'away days' which are widely found to be effective in facilitating team-building and a sense of corporate identity.

More broadly, there is a strong consensus among middle manager and more junior staff that transfer HAs value their staff more highly than predecessor LA housing departments. In combination with a commitment to a 'more professional' approach to housing management, this is usually reflected by a substantially greater commitment to staff training. The main exception here is the transfer landlords set up to take on ex-Scottish Homes stock. These organisations are descended from an agency which was already a 'single function' body seen as having been substantially committed to staff development. Consequently, the step-change improvement in access to training experienced by former LA staff now working for transfer HAs is not reflected here.

Particularly among English transfer landlords, the setting up of relatively small single purpose organisations largely carved out of much larger multi-functional bodies has been experienced as highly liberating by staff familiar with the working environment of predecessor councils. Aspirations to exploit new freedoms so as to provide improved customer services and to portray commitment to performance culture are sometimes reflected by the adoption of mission statements such as: "We aim to provide a service which is not just excellent, but legendary" (case study HA), and the creation of managerial post titles such as 'group manager, outstanding customer services' (case study HA).

By comparison with predecessor organisations, transfer landlords are generally seen as less hierarchical in their operation – irrespective of

any actual change in the number of managerial tiers. This partly involves greater delegation of managerial responsibility. Of at least equal importance is the efforts typically made to encourage lower-ranking staff to think in innovative and entrepreneurial ways rather than seeing their roles as simply to implement managerial instructions. Allied to this, middle and senior managers are generally found to be significantly more accessible than their former landlord counterparts, as well as being more receptive to ideas put forward by junior staff. Such changes are, of course, particularly marked in the case of estate- or neighbourhood-level partial transfer organisations carved out of large landlords. For ex-Scottish Homes staff, for example, the contrast between the managerial remoteness of the pre-transfer regime and the small self-contained structure of the transfer landlord was seen as stark.

The relatively 'inclusive' style of management favoured by transfer HAs is, perhaps, exemplified by the large-scale job evaluation exercise which was carried out in Year 3 of one case study landlord's existence. The exercise was prompted by the need to take account of the substantial changes in workloads and responsibilities since transfer. Staff at all levels were involved in job evaluation assessments and decisions. This approach was seen by staff as much more thorough, credible and fair than the comparable process as carried out within the predecessor council.

The setting up of staff forums to promote vertical communication between management and staff is another initiative often favoured by transfer HAs. While such bodies may involve official trades union representation, they are partly intended to allow for the fact that union membership is often fairly low and to afford staff direct access to the chief executive on a regular and semi-formal basis. This is reflected by the parallel study finding that the proportion of transfer HA staff reporting that their employer provides opportunities for them to articulate 'how they feel about how things affect them at work' is 21 percentage points higher than the public sector norm and 19% higher than the comparable figure for LA staff (Taper et al, 2003, para 3.14).

For the staff themselves, developments of this kind tend to be seen as highly positive and contributing to a more satisfying experience of work. At the same time, it seems that the degree of culture change typically alienates a small proportion of transferred staff, leading to a limited staffing 'shakeout' in the first year of a transfer HA's existence.

Salary structure and mechanisms

A widely held perception – in some instances exploited by anti-transfer campaigners – is that stock transfer tends to create increased salary differentials. Again, this would be consistent with the NPM stress on providing greater managerial incentives. In practice, only a bare majority of transfer landlords covered by our postal survey (56%) confirmed that the current salary differential between a housing officer and a 'second tier' manager was greater than that between a housing officer and the housing director in the pre-transfer housing department[3]. It is, however, notable that more than 40% of transfer landlords reported having maintained or reduced pre-transfer salary differentials on this basis.

Where salary differentials had increased, this generally tended to reflect changes taking place under the HA regime rather than solely at the time of the transfer itself.

Case study evidence reveals a diversity of approaches to setting pay. Some transfer HAs have retained formal linkages with the LA pay round so that cost of living increases are pegged to national settlements in the council sector. Increasingly, however, such links are being terminated as transfer landlords develop more customised and, arguably, more 'business-like' mechanisms. One case study association, for example, is planning a business plan RPI-linked increase complemented by a 'profit share' element connected with organisational performance in the previous year.

Many transfer landlords have toyed with the idea of performance-related pay, although some of those introduced have subsequently been

determined as inappropriate and scrapped. While some board members favour such approaches, senior managers and human resources professionals in particular are often sceptical as to their alleged benefits, seeing them as potentially both divisive and bureaucratic. Such systems rarely seem to command widespread support among staff and their introduction often provokes dissent.

Case study evidence, therefore, suggests that performance-related pay experiments are often short-lived. The message here is slightly at variance with the implication of Taper et al's report that 'appraisal-related' pay systems are relatively common among transfer HAs (Taper et al, 2003, para 3.71). Irrespective of performance-related pay, however, pay structures in the new landlords are often more flexible than is generally the case in local government. In two case study HAs, for example, managers had the power to recommend staff for 'exceptional increases' (beyond the 'top of their grade') in recognition of 'exceptional performance'.

More consumerist?

Most transfer HAs have substantial tenant representation among board members (see Chapter 5), and central government believes that stock transfer can bring about a more customer-focused service (see Chapter 2). It cannot, however, be assumed that transfer landlords' approach is necessarily any more consumerist than that of their predecessor organisations. Senior managers in a number of case study HAs stressed the challenge posed by the need to re-educate transferred staff in what was, initially at least, a new way of thinking. "Our constant message to staff", commented one interviewee, "is that tenants are customers and it's the tenants that pay the wages".

However, the transfer landlord view that they have replaced a paternalistic LA (or Scottish Homes) culture with a much more customer-focused approach seems to be borne out by the limited evidence gathered in this study from tenant board members and other tenant 'representatives'. In some case study HAs a key aspect of this change was the replacement of a 'no' culture with a 'yes' culture. In one case study HA, for example, the culture of the

---

[3] This comparison allows for the fact that a HA chief executive's responsibilities are, in some respects, wider than those of a LA housing director; that is, it is intended as a 'like for like' comparison of pre-transfer and current arrangements.

organisation was seen as having changed to a 'let's find a reason to say yes rather than no' ethos. In another, an interviewee reported "we are light years better at changing the 'no' culture to a 'yes' culture".

It should, of course, be acknowledged that the consumerist ethic has been gaining ground in the LA sector over the past decade, not least in response to 'top-down' pressure exerted through the requirements of the Best Value regime. However, testimony of case study transfer HA staff depicts transfer as typically ushering in a step-change in this aspect of organisational culture. Similarly, the widespread awareness of business plan imperatives seems likely to inculcate a perception of tenants as consumers to an extent unlikely to be paralleled among housing staff of remaining landlord LAs.

Evolution of organisational culture

Transfer HAs are generally 'carved out' of predecessor landlords, in that most of the staff initially employed had simply transferred across from the old to the new landlord body. To what extent had identified changes in organisational culture taken place in the immediate aftermath of transfer as opposed to coming about through subsequent evolution? In an attempt to address this issue, respondents were asked to consider a series of propositions loosely associated with 'good practice' in organisational management – broadly relating to staff empowerment, teamwork and transparency (see Table 9). Respondents were asked to what extent these propositions held true before transfer, one year after transfer and currently. It should be borne in mind that the period between '1 year after transfer' and 'currently' will have varied between two and 11 years.

Respondents were asked to score each proposition within a 1 to 5 range, where 5 represented 'strong agreement' and 1 represented 'strong disagreement'. Table 9 sets out the results from this exercise, comparing the mean scores recorded in respect of each proposition at the three specified times. In aggregate, responses tend to show a perceived temporal progression towards 'strong agreement' in respect of all the propositions – that is, average scores tend towards 5 from column 1 to column 3.

Table 9: English transfer HAs: views on the evolution of organisational culture

Proposition	In the housing department immediately pre-transfer	In the association	
		1 year after the transfer	Currently
	Average score (max 5)	Average score (max 5)	Average score (max 5)
Organisational aims and objectives are/were widely known and shared throughout the organisation	2.7	3.8	4.6
Staff feel/felt free to raise actual or potential difficulties and problems, confident that they will be/would be addressed	2.5	3.5	4.2
Non-conforming behaviour is/was not tolerated in the organisation	3.2	3.6	3.8
Teamwork plays/played a noticeable part in planning and setting standards	2.8	3.6	4.5
Managers and staff work/worked collaboratively to solve problems	2.9	3.8	4.4
Managers exercise/exercised flexible leadership according to situations	2.6	3.9	4.3
Organisational values are clear and explicit	2.6	4.0	4.7
Middle management and staff are/were encouraged to participate in decision making and policy	2.6	3.8	4.6
Staff roles are/were clear throughout the organisation	3.1	3.7	4.3
There is/was a high degree of trust between people within the organisation	2.8	3.7	4.1

It must, of course, be appreciated that these results are based on entirely subjective opinions on the part of respondents who were usually chief executives or other senior managers. They are likely to have some degree of vested interest in presenting changes in organisational practices and culture to suggest a 'progression towards good practice'. In general, however, the case study interviews with staff at a variety of levels within each subject HA seemed broadly confirmative of the general picture.

Interestingly, staff members in at least two of the longer-established case study HAs reported that there had been some recent retrenchment towards a 'LA style' of operation. Whereas the initial experience of operating as a HA had been of decision making becoming vastly quicker and more flexible, things had later tended to slip back somewhat towards a bureaucratic approach. In one case, this was plausibly attributed to the increased burden of regulation since the early 1990s, limiting the scope for discretionary action without the need to refer to formal procedural guidance. Another assertion was that, in forming a group structure, decision making had become somewhat more remote from operational staff.

Leaders and leadership

Notwithstanding the generalisations above, there are clearly very substantial contrasts in organisational cultures within the transfer HA cohort. This is probably influenced, in part, by the length of time that has elapsed since set-up. As time passes, the proportion of staff inherited from the predecessor landlord inevitably falls, and the organisation itself becomes increasingly attuned to the new regulatory regime. However, while this may generally hold true, it is far from immutable. In a number of case studies involving longer-established landlords, for example, early experiments with a private sector-style managerial approach (for example, performance-related pay) had later been abandoned.

In influencing the culture of an organisation, the priorities and personalities of chief executives can be even more important in a HA than in a LA. This was demonstrated particularly starkly in two case studies where the regimes of successive chief executives were seen by staff as akin to

chalk and cheese. One of these examples involved two leaders who, while each being highly respected, had taken the organisation in entirely different directions. The first phase had been characterised by development-led expansion, the deliberate weakening of ties to the home authority, and a relatively autocratic style of internal management. The second phase had been one of consolidation, renewal of relationships with the 'parent LA', and the development of a more consensual internal management style. In this instance, therefore, the passage of time did not appear to have resulted in a linear distancing of the association from its LA creator (see Chapter 7), or in the adoption of a 'private sector' culture.

In the other notable example of contrasting styles of successive chief executives, the replacement of an 'autocratic, hierarchical and secretive' leader led to the introduction of a more progressive, egalitarian approach and this was seen as having had a fundamental effect on the culture of the organisation as a whole.

Overview

Much of the evidence here – for example in relation to mission statements, post titles and adoption of 'business-speak' – refers to 'surface manifestations' of organisational culture. At the same time, however, the corroborative testimony of case study landlord staff at many levels suggests that ways of working and modes of thinking have changed in quite fundamental respects in many transfer HAs from those common in predecessor bodies.

5

Governance

Introduction

Many of the debates over the merits of stock transfer have revolved around governance and accountability issues. As noted in Chapter 2, a significant change in the national policy framework in England came in 1996 when it became permissible to establish transfer HAs under the local housing company model where there is equal representation for tenants, council nominees and 'independents'.

Based on case study and other evidence, this chapter looks at the way that governance arrangements are set up, function and evolve in transfer HAs.

Management board size and constituency representation

Board size

Housing Corporation guidance recommends that transfer HA management boards should contain between seven and 18 members (Housing Corporation, 1998a, p 16). In practice, the norm tends to be around 16 to 18, although there is some tendency for longer-established associations to have smaller boards (see Table 10). Sixty-two per cent of pre-1993 whole stock transfer HAs in England have 15 or fewer members, with eight organisations having less than 14. The larger boards, which tend to be the norm among more recently established landlords, probably reflect the application of the local housing company model, and post-transfer councils' common aspiration for cross-party representation.

It should be borne in mind that the figures set out in Table 10 show the 2001 composition of transfer HA boards. While most of these reflect decisions at the time of set-up, some will have been subsequently altered. For example, there is limited evidence suggesting a net tendency towards the reduction of management board size – at least in England; 34% of postal survey respondents reported a smaller number of board members in 2002 as compared with the immediate post-transfer position. Twenty-seven per cent of respondents, however, had seen their boards expand.

Table 10: Transfer HAs in existence in 2001: size of management boards

Era of establishment	Number of board member places						
	≤14	15	16	17	18	19+	Total
Pre-1994	8	5	3	3	0	2	21
1994-97	4	2	3	10	8	6	33
Post-1996	15	4	14	15	12	14	74
Total	27	11	20	28	20	22	128

Source: Housing Corporation registration data (unpublished)

Case study evidence suggests a fairly widespread aspiration among transfer HA senior managers in England in favour of smaller management boards. Mainly in the interests of more streamlined decision making and a greater focus on strategic rather than operational issues, chief executives of three of our 12 case study HAs favoured reducing membership of their main boards from 18 to 12. In at least two of these cases, however, the proposal was opposed by the LA and/or the majority of board members. Because constitutions generally require a minimum of 75% board member support for such changes, they cannot be implemented without the consent of members of all three 'constituency interest groups'.

The trend towards shrinking boards among English transfer HAs does not appear to be reflected in Scotland. This partly results from the fact that boards, as originally established, tend to have been considerably smaller here. Even in 2001, with eight of the 11 (73%) Scottish landlords responding to our postal survey reporting having expanded board membership since set-up, the commonest board size was 10 to 12 members rather than the 16 to 18 seen in England. In part, at least, this contrast probably reflects the fact that – with most landlords having been created from Scottish Homes rather than LA transfers – there will have been no expectation of a substantial council input into association governance.

Case study evidence suggests that the expansion of some Scottish transfer HA management boards may reflect the creation of additional spaces to accommodate (mainly ex-RTB) property owners – some of whom may receive management services from the transfer HA. One of our case study landlords – WESLO – had expanded its board by converting to local housing company format and inviting council representation (despite the fact

that the original stock transfer had been from Scottish Homes, not from a LA).

Constituency representation

As illustrated by Table 11, most transfer associations are set up so that a specific number of management board places are reserved for designated groups – for example tenants and councillors. In England this is the norm among all categories of transfer landlords, irrespective of whether they were set up under the post-1996 'local housing company' model. In most cases, therefore, changes to representation would necessitate constitutional amendments (see above).

The governance arrangements adopted by transfer landlords vary considerably by era of set-up, and by jurisdiction (England or Scotland). In general, however, transfer associations as a class are distinct from traditional HAs in that tenants and councillors are more significantly represented on management boards. Both groups are represented on all but a handful of boards in England (see Table 12).

According to Housing Corporation registration data, tenants make up some 26% of all English transfer HA board members. While this falls slightly short of the National Housing Federation's recent estimate of 'over a third' (NHF, 2002b), it is clearly substantial. And while it is difficult to relate this figure directly to comparable data for traditional HAs, it seems highly likely that it is far higher. At the start of the last decade, for example, it was estimated that among associations across Britain as a whole, only 40% of associations had *any* tenant board members, and the proportion of board members who were tenants was 'at best' 12% (Kearns, 1990, cited in Kearns, 1997). Given the

Table 11: Transfer landlords: rules on board member representation

| Whether association's rules reserve specific numbers of management board places for designated groups | England | | | | Scotland |
| | Whole stock transfers | | | | |
	1988–96	1997–99	Partial transfers	All	
Yes	16	7	6	29	7
No	6	3	0	9	7
Total number of respondents	22	10	6	38	14

Table 12: Stock transfer HAs in existence in England (2001)

a) Proportionate representation of tenant board members by era of HA establishment (number of HAs)

Era of establishment	% of tenant board members					
	0	1–20	21–33	34–50	>50	Total
Pre-1993	0	12	9	0	0	21
1993-96	0	12	19	1	1	33
Post-1996	3	2	59	9	1	74
All	3	26	87	10	2	128

Source: Housing Corporation registration data (unpublished)

b) Proportionate representation of council nominee members by era of HA establishment (number of HAs)

Era of establishment	% of tenant board members					
	0	1–20	21–33	34–50	>50	Total
Pre-1993	2	15	3	1	0	21
1993-96	0	28	5	0	0	33
Post-1996	3	14	50	7	0	74
All	5	57	58	8	0	128

Source: Housing Corporation registration data (unpublished)

known tradition of tenant governance among associations in Scotland (see below), the England-only figures would have been considerably lower than these.

Tenant board members have a particularly prominent role among transfer associations set up in Scotland. Here, official attitudes towards the proportion of 'non-independent' members on the boards of transfer landlords differed from those south of the border. Consequently, the concept of tenant-controlled associations was already a familiar one and there was no regulatory resistance to this. Half of all Scottish transfer HA board members are tenants and 55% of transfer landlords have tenant majority boards. By comparison, some 45% of traditional associations in Scotland are 'tenant controlled' (Communities Scotland regulatory data, unpublished). In most cases, however, these are small in size. If the two cohorts (transfer and non-transfer HAs) are matched for stock numbers, the proportion of stock transfer bodies with tenant-controlled boards is about double that of conventional associations.

While local housing company-style management boards have been allowed in England only since 1996, it has always been customary for transfer HA boards to involve council nominees as well

as tenants (see Table 12[b]). Scottish figures directly comparable to those for English transfer HAs shown in Table 12(b) are unavailable. However, postal survey evidence confirms that councillor representation is generally less common. Only seven of the 14 responding HAs (50%) reported that any councillors sat on their management board. And in no case did representation exceed two. In overall terms, nevertheless, it is probable that councillor participation is greater than among non-transfer associations in Scotland.

Board operation

The role of council nominees

Almost universally, councils invited to nominate HA board members interpret this as referring to sitting councillors. Initially following a transfer, nominees are often leading councillors keen to contribute to organisational governance. Over time, however, transfer landlords commonly report that the calibre of council nominees declines alongside the council's corporate interest in their association (or in housing issues, more generally). In some cases, this process also seems to reflect a gradually dawning appreciation that transfer HAs are independent bodies and cannot be seen as 'an arm of the council' subject to its continued dominance. Rochester and Hutchison (2002, p 17) report observing "two extreme kinds of [LA] reaction to the transfer process". Some see the transfer as marking the termination of their responsibility for housing in any form, while "others [are] 'in denial': their representatives on the transfer association board continued to act as if little has changed".

Echoing this latter sentiment, many of our (English) case study HAs had experienced an initial period where council 'representatives' seemed to believe that association board meetings ought to be conducted just as those of the predecessor LA: stances on any question would, for example, be determined by reference to party decisions as agreed in advance. Councillor board members are often said to find it difficult to adapt to a role appropriate in this context – that is, where board members operate as individuals rather than on a 'mandation' basis, where decisions need to be arrived at in a non-political way, and where the details of debate are confidential. In one case study association a 'communications protocol' had been established as a guide for councillor board members confused about their respective loyalties. What is seen as inappropriately assertive behaviour on the part of councillor board members in the early life of some transfer HAs tends to generate alliances between tenant 'representatives' and 'independents'.

As far as council nominees are concerned, a common complaint is that they have a poor board attendance record. According to (unpublished) Housing Corporation regulatory data, however, there seems to be little substance to this. In 2000/01, for instance, the average number of board meetings attended by councillor 'representatives' on English transfer associations was 5.2 – as against 5.5 for 'independents' and 5.6 for tenants.

A more well-founded complaint seems to be that council representation lacks continuity and that this impedes efforts to train nominees and to inculcate 'HA values and norms'. Certainly, our own survey data confirms that councillor representation lacks stability. For example, over a third of transfer associations in England (36%) reported experiencing 'high turnover' on the part

of this group, double the proportion reporting 'high turnover' of tenant board members.

Council nominees' typical position as sitting councillors means that their term of HA office may be interrupted by a change in party control, by personal electoral defeat or simply the operation of traditional 'rotational' systems for determining council representation on outside bodies. To counter such problems, one case study HA had recently secured council agreement to three-year terms for its board member nominees. Another solution might be for councils to nominate people other than sitting councillors – and, indeed, Housing Corporation rules allow for the possibility that nominees might be council staff or former councillors (Housing Corporation, 1998a). Only in one of our nine English case studies, however (a partial transfer association in inner London), did the council routinely nominate officers among its 'representatives'.

While some councillor nominees clearly see their role as being to represent their authority in a semi-political sense, the view that they should speak for the council in more official, corporate, terms is quite uncommon. In one of our case studies, LA officers continued to brief councillor board 'representatives' on a regular basis more than 10 years after the transfer. This involved the council's housing, finance and planning staff. A particular focus of such briefings was ensuring that nominees appreciated the financial implications of HA decisions in the context of the prevailing funding framework. It would seem that such practices reflect the continuing close relationship between the council and its transfer HA partner and that they are unusual in the wider scheme of things.

Although it is not unknown, it is unusual for council nominees to take the role of transfer HA board chairperson. One consideration here is the need to ensure that organisational independence is apparent as well as real. An additional issue for some is that this might be seen as inappropriate given a transfer HA's development and/or managerial activity outside the boundaries of its original LA.

Although turnover of council nominee board members is typically rather high, case study evidence tends to corroborate the earlier research finding that councillors elected to HA boards often 'go native' to the extent that they progressively transfer their prime loyalty from the council to the association (Mullins, 1996). This is consistent with the more recent finding that councillor HA board members commonly see their role as "representing the HA to the LA" (Audit Commission, 2002, p 44).

Particularly among longer-established associations, there is some evidence of a tendency towards reducing councillor representation – in some cases in favour of increased tenant membership. Transfer HA senior managers interpret this as reflecting a gradually declining sense of LA ownership of their associations, as well as a growing shortage of councillors willing to accept nomination. This, in turn, may be due to the shrinking number of councillors with fond memories of (pre-transfer) housing committee membership.

More broadly, some chief executives of post-1996 transfer associations in England consider the local housing company model to be a recipe for factionalism – for example, in the immediate post-set-up tendency for tenant and/or council 'representatives' to operate as a bloc – for example, each 'group' coordinating its approach through an organised pre-meeting and voting collectively. One chief executive of a case study HA viewed The Housing Corporation's advocacy of the local housing company model as being in direct conflict with its *Modernising governance* (Housing Corporation, 2001) recommendations.

The role of tenant board members[4]

Particularly in earlier transfers, the recruitment of tenant board members at set-up has sometimes been a fairly ad hoc process, largely reflecting the lack of existing tenant representative structures under the predecessor landlords concerned. More recently, such processes have often involved elections from properly constituted tenants' forums and federations. Some of the longer-established transfer HAs have set up such frameworks since their own creation and have drawn on them to refresh tenant board member representation.

---

[4] The role of transfer association tenant board members is examined in a separate Joseph Rowntree Foundation-sponsored study (Reid, 2003: forthcoming).

Whether achieved through discretionary selection or following from tenant elections, some transfer HAs have attempted the incorporation of 'transfer sceptics' as tenant board members. While this is often effective, it can be a high-risk strategy leading, in one case study, for example, to board member conflict and the eventual forcible ejection of the 'troublesome' individual concerned.

Tenant board chairs, common in Scotland, are not unknown in England but some associations take the view that this role would place a tenant in an 'over-exposed' position. Another view is that tenant board members tend to 'fight shy' of taking on chairing roles because of the intimidating nature of financial management responsibility. Tenant chairpersonship is also believed by some senior managers (pre-local housing company associations) to be contrary to The Housing Corporation rules. In one (local housing company) case study association it was reported that the Corporation had instructed the association to replace a tenant chair with an independent as part of a 'recovery plan' to reassure funders following the association's breach of a financial covenant.

Tenant board members are valued in giving legitimacy to transfer associations and many make a substantial input into board discussions and decisions. It is, however, appreciated that the tenant board member training needs are often substantial, both in terms of the unfamiliar technical complexities of association management, and in terms of building confidence sufficient to facilitate full participation in board deliberations. Most case study HAs reported having provided extensive training to tenant board members, both to induct them into their new role, and to build on this subsequently.

Despite the volume of training made available, however, it is often perceived that tenant board members play only a limited role in board decision making. In one case study HA, for example, a senior manager reported that tenant board members' role had been very limited, with "several of them never opening their mouths once in four years". In another association, there was concern that, despite substantial support, tenant board members remained "very much the silent partners" in terms of contribution to the decision-making process.

Managers in a number of case study HAs voiced frustration at their inability to help tenant board members transcend a perception of their proper role as representing tenant views over 'minor issues of repairs and maintenance'. There is a case to be made that such perceptions are sometimes perpetuated by HAs themselves. One large transfer HA which has set up a group structure, for example, has seen it as inappropriate to create tenant member places on the main group board because of the intended focus of this board on corporate strategy rather than operational matters.

Across England, 20 transfer HAs (two in England and 18 in Scotland) are 'tenant controlled' (that is, tenants account for the majority of board members)[5]. Among the chief executives of the 14 such HAs responding in our postal survey, six believed that this factor had no "discernible influence on (their) association's activities and/or strategic policy making". Some of the examples of 'tenant-influenced' strategic decisions cited by the eight respondents who took the opposite view were somewhat unconvincing. The more apparently plausible instances included:

- "demolish rather than modernise";
- "provision of local offices in areas with low stock numbers";
- "planned improvement programme balances technical needs … with tenant comfort issues".

There is also a view – as expounded by the Scottish Federation of HAs – that tenant board members are unlikely to favour geographical diversification (that is, expansion of stockholdings outwith the association's 'home area'). The validity of this perception is explored in Chapter 6.

---

[5] While Housing Corporation registration rules embody a strong preference for the formation of boards composed of tenants, council nominees and 'independents' in equal numbers, the opportunity for tenants and/or council nominees to be represented in larger numbers is left open if there are compelling reasons for such arrangements. Both Scottish Homes and its successor body, Communities Scotland, have actively promoted the establishment of tenant-majority transfer associations, although there is now an expectation that LA transfers will involve 'local housing company-style' governance structures.

However, while these findings might seem to challenge the belief that the 'constituency' background of board members matters, the linkage between board make-up and strategic direction is not the only relevant issue. As Kearns (1997) points out, there are a number of arguments in favour of the view that the board representation of various 'interest groups' is significant, namely the organisation's:

- self-identity
- reputation
- legitimacy
- effectiveness
- security and reassurance.

The general thrust here is that the 'constituency mix' of board members is important in symbolic terms, even if any clear policy direction associated with those from particular 'constituencies' is difficult to identify.

The role of 'independent' board members

Underlying some of the views discussed above is the clear implication that senior managers in many transfer HAs often see the need to work with tenant and councillor board members as something of an encumbrance. Independent board members drawn, for example, from business, legal or surveying backgrounds are often seen as having a 'refreshingly non-political' approach.

Independent board members are often recruited through local employers, although open advertising is increasingly being used. Such processes often involve shortlisting and interviewing against specific 'competencies'. Some associations are also encouraging councils to assess potential board member nominees against such requirements.

Transfer HAs set up as subsidiaries of existing HAs form a special case with respect to 'independent' board members. To maintain linkage between the group parent and group member, the former may nominate some or all of these members.

Overall, both case study and survey evidence suggests that 'independent' board member turnover is somewhat lower than among either tenants or council 'representatives'. Their typically long-serving status may help to explain the observation that, in England at least, board chairs are usually occupied by 'independents'.

Evolution of board operation

In general, factionalism and other inappropriate board member behaviour tends to decline with the passage of time as all parties become more familiar with the new regime (or resign their membership if unable to do so). In some cases, however, the process is stimulated by regulatory intervention. Two of our case study HAs, for example, had seen such action. In one instance, for example, board members attended an away-from-office weekend convened by regulator-appointed consultants (and from which association officers were excluded). At this event board members reviewed their role and the need to re-establish the board's supremacy as the accountable body. This was felt to have been useful by those attending and to have contributed to developing a more appropriate relationship between officers and board members. Similar positive outcomes were reported in the context of the other case study HA subject to regulator action.

More generally, there is a view that central government's post-1996 enthusiasm for the local housing company model is a 'concession' to encourage acceptance of the transfer option among both councillors and tenants. Given the sometimes problematic working relationships within local housing company boards, there could be an argument that such structures can be sub-optimal in narrow efficiency terms. This reasoning would suggest that, over time, there might be pressure to reshape board constitutions in pursuit of more 'business-like' structures. As yet, however, there is little evidence of such a tendency.

6

Housing management

Introduction

As discussed in Chapter 3, transfer HAs (in England at least) have, over time, tended to move towards more centralised, functionally specialised organisational structures – a trend with clear implications for housing management practice.

More broadly, however, how is the institutional status and organisational ethos of stock transfer landlords reflected through their approach to housing management? Walker's arguments (1998) (as cited in Chapter 3) would suggest that transfer associations – being typically much more heavily indebted than conventional associations – might adopt a particularly 'hard-nosed' operational style. In Scotland, at least, there is a belief on the part of the regulator that transfer associations have been in the vanguard of sector-wide moves towards more commercially minded approaches and that in this way they have impacted on the overall culture of the sector. This echoes the point made by Pollitt et al (1998) cited in Chapter 2.

After briefly discussing the immediate impact of transfer on formal housing management policies, this chapter looks at the extent to which the typically highly indebted and 'business plan-focused' status of transfer HAs gives rise to a 'tough' style of housing management. It examines the measures that transfer HAs see as demonstrating a more consumerist approach than their predecessor landlords (see Chapter 4). And, picking up from the discussion in that chapter on attempts to foster 'performance cultures', it goes on to investigate the evidence available to support the contention that this delivers tangible results.

Impact of transfer on housing management practice

Almost universally, the transfer HA experience has involved moving to a regime where policies and procedures are considerably more documented than was previously the case. This is often simply a matter of responding to regulatory expectations by formalising what are already familiar approaches. In other instances, newly documented policies have been influenced by the approaches of group parent associations.

The policy *change* most frequently mentioned by English HAs as resulting from transfer is the scrapping of local connection rules for waiting list applicants – an amendment routinely required by The Housing Corporation. Other than this, the general view seems to be that housing management policies change very little as a result of transfer, although it is commonly asserted that familiar policies are 'implemented more efficiently' – an issue to which we return below.

According to our postal survey, two thirds of transfer landlords (in both England and Scotland) introduced housing management policies and procedures in the immediate post-transfer period which 'differed significantly from those operated by their predecessor landlord'. In both jurisdictions, however, this proportion was higher among recently formed landlords (83% of post-1996 landlords compared with only 56% of 1988-96 landlords). This probably reflects the increasingly detailed 'menu of required policies' issued by regulators to newly established transfer associations moving from the informally regulated LA sector to the formally regulated HA sector.

Specific examples of 'significant post-transfer changes in housing management policies and practices' cited by respondents included:

(a) appeals procedure
(b) area boards with local control
(c) charging economic service charge
(d) decentralised service delivery
(e) end use of distraint for rent arrears
(f) equal opportunities policy
(g) local lettings scheme
(h) money/lettings advice
(i) nominations agreements with LA
(j) plain English policy – no jargon or legalese
(k) proactive management
(l) tenant consultation
(m) unlimited succession rights.

While this list is fairly diverse, a number of items (a, b, d, j and l) could be portrayed as consistent with the development of a more 'customer-focused' style of operation. There is little obvious sign here of any acknowledgement that management has become more 'property-centred' and less 'welfare-centred', a tendency we might expect to find among organisations moving from a risk-sheltered to a risk-exposed situation.

At the same time, it can be seen that transfer landlords are inclined to portray themselves as operating a tighter – but not necessarily a tougher – style of housing management. What objective evidence exists as to whether transfer landlords operate a 'hard-line' housing management style? Perhaps the best single

yardstick here is a landlord's eviction rate – that is, the number of evictions per thousand homes in management. The (highly arguable) hypothesis would be that transfer HAs' eviction rates will exceed those of other social landlords – not only because of their greater exposure to risk, but also because, unlike LAs, they do not have to consider the impact of evictions on homelessness.

Unfortunately, it is not possible to compare eviction rates of transfer associations with their predecessor LAs, or, as far as England is concerned, to contrast transfer bodies and LAs as classes of landlords. However, a comparison between transfer landlords and conventional HAs, and between transfer landlords and LAs in Scotland, lends no support at all to the contention that the former are habitually 'tough landlords' (see Figures 1 and 2).

It is also interesting to note the lack of any obvious correlation between eviction rates and effectiveness in rent collection. In Scotland, for example, in 2000/01 transfer associations were almost on a par with conventional associations in terms of the value of arrears as a proportion of rent due, yet their eviction rate was well under half that of their non-transfer counterparts (see Figure 2). In England the comparison is even starker: while transfer associations typically record much lower eviction rates (see Figure 1), they significantly out-perform their 'conventional' counterparts on this measure of housing management performance. In 2000/01, for

Figure 1: HA eviction rates: England (1999/2000)

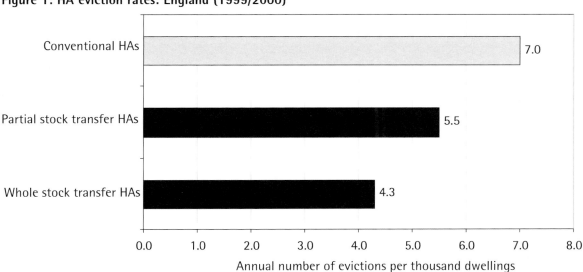

Source: Housing Corporation regulatory returns (2002)

Figure 2: HA and LA eviction rates: Scotland (2000/01)

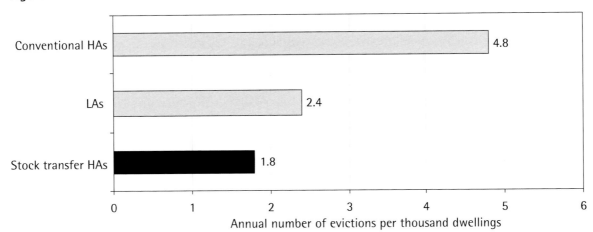

Note: LA data relate to 2001/02 (annual equivalent figure based on first two quarters).
Source: Communities Scotland regulatory returns (2001) and Scottish Executive Housing Trends Statistical Series

example, they collected 96.8% of rent due as against a sector-wide score of 94.8% (see Table 13).

Case study evidence sheds additional light on this issue. For most of the 12 associations, rent arrears policy was seen as little different from that under the predecessor landlord – indeed, in one instance it was argued to be more relaxed.

In three case studies, however, there was an explicit recognition by staff that policy and implementation had become more 'hard-line' in comparison with the predecessor LA. In two instances, for example, the threshold for the

issue of notices seeking possession (NSPs) had been reduced from six weeks' rent under the former LA landlord to four weeks' rent under the successor regime. In one of these HAs, staff described their approach as 'fair but ruthless'.

It may well be significant that two of the three 'now more hard-line' HAs were partial transfer associations which had taken on run-down estates where there was said to be a strong pre-transfer culture of rent non-payment. Both of these HAs saw the need to change this culture as a key challenge and one that required a clear demonstration of the landlord's resolve, at least initially. A series of evictions carried through by

Table 13: HAs in England: 2000/01 median performance indicator scores compared

Performance indicator	Transfer HAs	Non-transfer HAs					All
		Large	London	South	Central	North	
Rent collected as % of rent collectable	96.8	93.7	92.9	95.4	93.9	94.8	**94.8**
Rent arrears as % of rent roll	3.3	7.1	7.6	4.8	6.5	5.3	**5.5**
Average re-let interval (days)	29	46	41	32	27	39	**33**
% of landlords offering repairs appointments	42	25	38	31	34	31	**35**
Tenants' satisfaction: overall landlord service (%)	81	79	80	86	83	80	**80**
Tenants' satisfaction: opportunities for participation (%)	64	56	62	66	64	59	**62**

Note: 'Transfer HAs' defined as whole stock transfer landlords only (partial transfer HAs incorporated within other 'peer groups').
Source: Raw data from Audit Commission and Housing Corporation performance indicator datasets (accessible at www.audit-commission.gov.uk and www.housingcorp.gov.uk)

one of these associations shortly after having taken on ownership was said to have evoked a sharp reaction in the form of organised protest on the part of residents. This was partly inspired by a widespread (although misinformed) belief that there had been no previous evictions on the estate for 15 years.

More broadly, there is evidence that transfer HAs are increasingly adopting less constrained definitions of 'housing management'. Because of its links with the wider issue of their involvement in 'community regeneration' – an aspect of 'functional diversification' – this issue is discussed in more detail in Chapter 7.

Stock transfer and housing management performance

Perhaps not surprisingly, transfer HA managers and staff generally argue that management performance has improved under the new regime as compared with the situation under the predecessor landlord. Tenant board members tend to agree. Case study interviewees generally ascribed such improvements to the new landlord's 'more professional' approach as a unified, single-purpose organisation removed from the party political arena.

Evidence has also been advanced to underpin an assertion that tenants, more widely, see transfer as having helped to generate better services. For example, Cobbold and Dean (2000) reported that overall 'satisfaction with landlord' rates were significantly higher among transfer HA tenants (85%) than among LA tenants (79%). More specifically, 38% of transferring tenants in this study believed that the quality of housing management had improved following transfer as compared with only 9% who believed the opposite to be true.

Case study evidence suggests that widespread 'local actor' perceptions of service improvements under post-transfer regimes are generally justified. Whether it is also true that such gains have created a cohort of landlords in a performance class of their own is, however, another matter. It might well be, for example, that the advances seen under transfer landlords are no greater than those occurring within the remaining LA sector. Some parties arguing the case that transfer results in measurable service improvement cite simple performance indicator score comparisons between LAs and transfer HAs as classes of landlord. For example, it is pointed out by the National Housing Federation that transfer HAs' management costs are typically 18% lower than those of their LA landlord counterparts. Similarly, average re-let intervals are shorter and rent collection rates higher (NHF, 2002b).

The national comparison shown in Table 14 (cols 2 and 3) only partially bears out the National Housing Federation's argument. Moreover, the comparison is of questionable value, given the predominance of larger landlords operating in more challenging conditions within the LA sector. A more 'like for like' comparison (see Table 14, columns 4 and 5) entirely eliminates any

Table 14: LAs and transfer HAs in England: 2000/01 median performance indicator scores compared

Performance indicator	England		South of England	
	LAs	Transfer HAs	District councils	Transfer HAs
Rent collected as % of rent collectable	96.9	96.8	97.6	96.7
Rent arrears as % of rent roll	2.8	3.3	2.5	3.3
Average re-let interval (days)	41	29	32.0	28.4
% of landlords offering repairs appointments	54	42	NA	NA
Tenants' satisfaction: overall landlord service (%)	79	81	82	82
Tenants' satisfaction: opportunities for participation (%)	58	64	65	68

Note: 'Transfer HAs' defined as whole stock transfer landlords only.

Source: Raw data from Audit Commission and Housing Corporation performance indicator datasets (accessible at www.audit-commission.gov.uk and www.housingcorp.gov.uk)

consistent message that one sector generally outperforms the other on these standard measures of housing management efficiency and effectiveness[6]. The comparison here takes account of the fact that the vast majority of transfer HAs operating in the South of England have taken on former district council stock. Second, the focus only on specific regions limits the range of housing market circumstances being encountered by the landlords involved. Few, if any, will be seriously troubled by low demand. And most will be managing stock primarily involving cottage-style estates rather than non-traditional housing.

Thus, while it may well be true that transfer HAs have improved their performance over and above the levels achieved by predecessor landlords, it may be that this has done little more than match performance improvement by remaining LA landlords. While this may be seen as unexpected, it is consistent with the findings of some previous studies. Looking at Scottish transfers, for example, Graham (1999) found that transfer brought no immediate bonus in terms of improved management performance as measured by key performance indicators. Similarly, Mullins et al's early evaluation of English transfers cautiously stated simply that "all aspects of the service appear to have been either maintained or improved following LSVT" (Mullins et al, 1995, p 59).

Further, while our findings may appear to conflict with Cobbold and Dean's (2000) tenant satisfaction evidence (see above), these authors conceded that a 'feel good' factor produced by major catch-up repairs programmes in the immediate post-transfer period can beneficially affect overall satisfaction scores at this stage. "There is evidence that tenant satisfaction ratings among LSVT tenants may decline once initial (and frequently extensive) improvements have been made to tenants' homes" (Cobbold and Dean, 2000, p 5).

It should be acknowledged that the indicators compared in Table 14 do not include repairs activity – undoubtedly the prime aspect of service delivery influencing tenants' judgements

on landlords' performance. It is possible, of course, that transfer HAs' repairs performance has improved substantially more than that of (comparable) LAs. And while it is not possible to compare repairs activity as in Table 14, the National Housing Federation reports that "the percentage of repairs completed within target times by transfer HAs improved by 12.4 per cent" (NHF, 2002b, p 4). Generally, however, while transfer HAs may be more tenant-influenced, tenant-friendly and consumerist in outlook, there is little hard evidence for the claim that they are 'higher performing' housing managers than LAs.

At the same time, Table 13 suggests that (whole stock) transfer HAs perform well in comparison with other HAs and, within the sector, to some extent set a standard for others to match. Similarly (whole stock) transfer landlords record significantly lower average unit management costs than non-transfer HAs. In 2001/02, for example, the respective figures were £10.45 and £12.47. This is in keeping with the argument that the former are, in Cobbold and Dean's terms, "a new breed of dynamic RSLs" (2000, p 6). In itself, however, it does not prove that transfer landlords are inherently more 'business-like' or 'efficient' than their non-transfer counterparts because the former clearly enjoy certain advantages over the latter, in particular, a typically more compact and sometimes more physically standardised stock, as well as greater scope for economies of scale. Only through an intensive and technically focused study could a more definitive conclusion be reached on this issue.

---

[6] Although it should be acknowledged that the different structure of the Housing Benefit regime as it relates to rent allowances rather than rent rebates inevitably appears to 'exaggerate' HA rent arrears.

7

Finance and development

Introduction

This chapter looks at transfer HAs' debt profile and its implications for their attitudes and activities, especially in relation to 'functional diversification': moves to develop activities away from an organisation's own core business and competencies, usually implying activities beyond traditional social landlord pursuits. It also analyses transfer landlords' approaches to new housing development in terms of its scale, location and tenure.

Business plan assumptions, and their implications

The primary declared motivation for stock transfer is the need to secure investment in social housing. And, since 1988, transfers have channelled £5.6 billion into repairs, improvement and new development in England alone (NHF, 2002b). Typically, an association takes out a loan to finance the initial transfer, with further funds being drawn down during its first few years of existence as it re-invests in the stock to complete a programme of 'catch-up repairs and improvements'. Some time later, with gradually increasing rental income, peak debt is passed and the association begins to generate revenue surpluses, thus transforming its overall financial position (see Figure 3).

The precise shape of a transfer HA's debt profile varies, of course, depending on its circumstances (for example, whether or not the pre-transfer stock has a net positive value) and on the terms of the deal agreed with between association and funder. It will also depend on the assumptions built into the HA business plan, for example, in relation to future rents, ongoing management and maintenance expenditure, and so on.

Figure 3: Debt profile for typical 'positive value' transfers

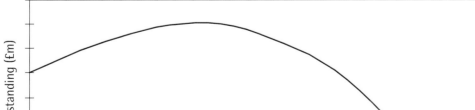
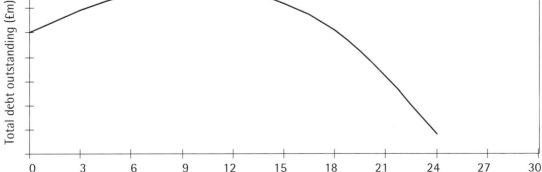

Source: The Housing Corporation (1998b)

A study of early transfer HAs suggested that income and expenditure projections built into original business plans for the first five years of the new associations' existence tended to be highly inaccurate (PIEDA, 1997). And, while transfer business planning has become more sophisticated over the years, it is still commonplace for such plans to need substantial revisions within a short time of set-up (see below). Because 'transfer promises', for example, on rents and catch-up repairs, are seen as sacrosanct, the newly created landlord usually has very limited room for manoeuvre if costs are higher than predicted and/or income is lower. This may place it in a very vulnerable position, particularly if the pressures of having to face up to unpalatable options cause stresses for a management board which has yet to 'gel' into a cohesive unit. One of our case study landlords, facing such a scenario, was taken into supervision by The Housing Corporation only a year after set-up. That nearly a fifth of transfer HAs have "given rise to serious [Housing Corporation] concerns in respect of their financial viability or governance" (NAO, 2003, p 23) illustrates that this is not a particularly unusual circumstance.

Some of the 'early cohort' transfer HAs were fortunate enough to experience benign economic conditions which led to their business plan expectations proving substantially over-cautious. While they may have been saddled with loans borrowed at relatively high rates of interest, many transfer landlords set up in the 1988-92 period benefited from the construction industry recession of the early 1990s which caused works tender prices to fall rapidly. Inflation, meanwhile, was running at higher than predicted levels. Given the link between rents and RPI , the outcome was higher than predicted income[7] in combination with lower than expected repairs costs. At the same time, rising public spending on housing provided largely unforeseen opportunities for the development of new housing (for example, through the 1992/93 Housing Market Package). And under the Corporation's strongly value-for-money-driven policy of this era, there was no impediment to the construction of housing remote from an association's 'home base'.

Business plans are working models, constantly in need of review and revision as economic and other circumstances change. Sometimes such revisions reflect advantageous developments of the kind described above. Often, however, early business plan revisions result in the need for belt-tightening rather than the reverse. All too often, defective stock condition assessments (sometimes in combination with underestimated works tender prices) lead to overoptimistic estimates of unit repair and improvement costs. In one of our case studies, for example, it became clear within months of transfer that unit costs were averaging 50% in excess of business plan estimates. The resulting enforced economies included re-phasing the refurbishment programme, integrating more activities with the group parent body and withdrawing from some 'community regeneration' commitments. In another instance, higher than anticipated refurbishment costs had prejudiced funding for planned new build housing for rent, leaving the association contemplating the possibility of developing at densities higher than envisaged and/or building for sale rather than rent.

Development of new housing

Facilitating the repair and upgrading of existing housing forms is by far the most significant factor motivating the stock transfer programme. Nevertheless, as mentioned in Chapter 2, some English transfers have been triggered, to a significant degree, by an aspiration to develop additional social housing.

In practice, virtually all transfer associations established in England before April 1999 had, by 2002, become active in new development. Among our postal survey respondents, only one association (a small partial transfer landlord) reported having no expectation of initiating new development. The 37 English transfer associations responding in our survey had, collectively, built over 20,000 homes. Given that these represent just over a third of all pre-1999 transfer landlords, our figure tallies closely with the National Housing Federation's global estimate for England of 48,000 homes built by all transfer associations (NHF, 2002b).

Nevertheless, as shown by Table 15, over two thirds of transfer HAs have experienced a net

---

[7] As reflected in PIEDA's (1997) observation of a common tendency for early transfer HAs to see rental income running ahead of original business plan projections.

Table 15: Transfer HAs established 1988-2001: net change in housing stock to 2002

	Loss			Gain				Number of
Period HA set up	>10%	5-10%	0-5%	0-5%	5-10%	10% +	Total	HAs
Early (1988-92)	7	13	20	13	11	36	100	45
Mid (1993-96)	11	46	35	4	0	4	100	46
Recent (1997-2001)	6	19	53	22	0	0	100	32
All	8	27	34	12	4	15	100	123

Source: Housing Corporation regulatory and statistical returns data (2002) and ODPM (2002) stock transfer listing

loss of housing since being set up. Even among the 'early' cohort, only 60% had, by 2002, developed and acquired more dwellings than they had lost. The main factor here is sitting tenant sales under the preserved RTB. In 2001/02, for example, transfer HAs sold around 7,000 homes in this way – approximately 1% of their total housing stock. And, with the increasing tendency for transfer in areas of shrinking demand for social housing, demolitions are also a significant factor. In 2001/02, transfer HAs demolished nearly 2,000 homes. Given that transfer HAs are currently developing or acquiring only around 6,000 homes annually, net stock losses are running at around 3,000 homes per year.

By comparison with their English counterparts, transfer HAs in Scotland have tended to be more focused on managing and improving their original stock rather than on developing new housing. Two thirds of pre-1999 transfer HAs had, by 2002, developed some new housing and (according to postal survey evidence) most of the others anticipated initiating a new build programme in the near future. At the same time, however, only four of 31 registered transfer HAs had managed to develop and acquire more dwellings than had lost (mainly through the preserved RTB). By 2002 Scottish transfer landlords were, collectively, managing 2% fewer homes than they had originally taken into ownership through transfers. For eight transfer landlords (a quarter of the total) net stock losses exceeded 10% of the number originally transferred.

The development drive

Virtually all transfer associations see themselves as active developers of new housing, as well as custodians of transferred stock. In part, this drive reflects the founding aspirations of LAs (see page 7). Nearly half of all pre-1999 transfer HAs in England were required to develop new housing under the stock transfer contract with their founding LA. Such circumstances are exemplified by East Lindsey District Council's expectation that its transfer HA partner, Linx Homes, would develop 400 new homes during the first five years after set-up in 1999.

In many cases, such aspirations have been backed by commitments (in certain instances written into transfer contracts) to provide funding (sometimes through 'recycling' transfer receipts) for a given period through LA Social Housing Grant (SHG) allocations[8]. In setting up its transfer to Hereward HA, for example, East Cambridgeshire District Council undertook to fund an association development programme of 50 houses per year for the first five years post-transfer. Generally, however, such agreements have been time-limited and transfer associations have increasingly found themselves needing to 'make a case' for any continuing 'priority treatment' by their home LAs (and, in some cases, competing with other associations for LA SHG allocations from other councils).

For most transfer associations there is also a development drive from within the organisation itself (rather than from the 'parent' LA). In part, this may reflect an ambition to integrate within the HA sector: "We do not want ourselves, nor other LA-sponsored HAs, to be seen as a separate breed. We seek integration with the existing HA movement" (former chief executive of a 1990 transfer association).

---

[8] With the recent abolition of LA SHG, such arrangements will, however, be discouraged to the extent that councils will no longer be able to reclaim from The Housing Corporation, capital funding of HAs.

More practically, transfer associations need to seek opportunities for growth merely to counteract stock losses through the preserved RTB enjoyed by pre-transfer tenants. Net erosion of stock is likely to generate higher unit management costs leading, in turn, to upward pressure on rents. In the long run, associations in this position may face pressure to merge with stronger partners, resulting in a potential loss of local identity and control. Motivated by such considerations, one case study association established in 1998 had recently adopted a development target of recovering the stock total at the original transfer by 2008.

A second practical impetus in favour of new development might arise from an association's wish to capitalise on the skills and expertise accumulated during the intense period of catch-up repairs and modernisation of transferred stock, typically experienced by transfer associations during their first five years. Emerging from this period an association could be expected to seek ways of maintaining its workforce. Case study evidence suggests that management boards, as well as senior managers, are often strongly committed to seeking new development opportunities.

Transfer landlords in Scotland differ from their English counterparts in that there has been no prospect of recycling capital receipts into new development and that, in general, opportunities for the construction of new housing have been much more limited. In the long term, this may prove problematic, since, like LAs, they face stock losses under the RTB, while having little opportunity to replace these losses. One of our Scottish case study landlords, WESLO, is also hamstrung in its post-transfer ability to access private finance due to being unregistered with Communities Scotland[9]. In this instance, partly through the establishment of a strong relationship with its main LA partner, the association has been able to develop or acquire significant new housing on a significant scale as a beneficiary of challenge funding under the New Housing Partnerships and Empty Homes programmes. A mortgage rescue scheme has also contributed. This example seems to illustrate a degree of creativity fostered by difficult circumstances.

Geographical diversification through new development

The majority of housing developed by transfer HAs is located within the 'home LA' of the association concerned. However, as shown in Figure 4, this varies substantially between England and Scotland, and between English

---

[9] As a result of the association's commitment to a governance structure in which senior managers sit on the organisation's management board and where the board chair is paid rather than voluntary.

Figure 4: Location of new housing developed by transfer HAs

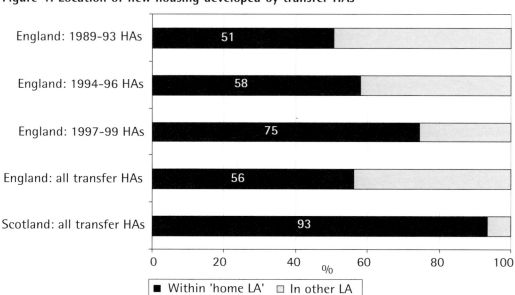

transfer landlords established in different periods. Virtually half the homes developed by the earliest group of English transfer HAs have been built outside 'home LA' boundaries. This proportion is substantially lower for more recently created landlords. In fact, the figures for the 1997-99 cohort (as shown in Figure 4) are heavily influenced by the activities of one association that has built more than half of its large output of new dwellings outside its original area of operation. A more revealing statistic is that only two of the 16 responding 1997-99 associations had built *any* homes outside their original area.

A number of the pre-1994 transfer landlords have become major regional players, with significant stockholdings in many LA areas. However, it can be seen from Figure 5 that most remain focused on a single LA area. For example, only two own stock in more than 20 LA areas while this is true of about a third of the non-transfer associations included in the graphic. Nevertheless, it might be assumed that wide-ranging geographical diversification within the transfer HA sub-sector is simply a matter of time. The evidence, however, suggests otherwise. Many 'early cohort' transfer associations quickly developed new housing on a scale far in excess of original business plan expectations, with much of this development taking place beyond the boundaries of their 'home LAs'. However, it is important to

appreciate that this expansion was facilitated by a specific combination of circumstances which is unlikely to recur. These included the co-existence of:

- falling works tender prices (at least in some regions);
- inflation at moderate levels (facilitating expanding rental income);
- rapidly rising public funding for HA investment until 1993/94;
- a strong Housing Corporation emphasis on competition relative to existing local presence;
- an absence of rent control.

For this reason, it would be mistaken to imagine that, given time, more recently created transfer landlords will inevitably come to emulate their longer-established counterparts by becoming significant regional players (unless they achieve this through mergers and/or group structure collaborations with existing HAs).

Another factor, as confirmed by case study evidence, is the constitutional difference between pre- and post-1996 transfer HAs. In general, the stronger board representation of tenants and council nominees on more recently created landlords seems to play in favour of a stronger local focus than was apparent among many 'early cohort' associations. In one post-1996 case study, a tenant board member's view was that "I

Figure 5: Geographical distribution of HA stock in 2001: transfer and non-transfer HAs compared[a]

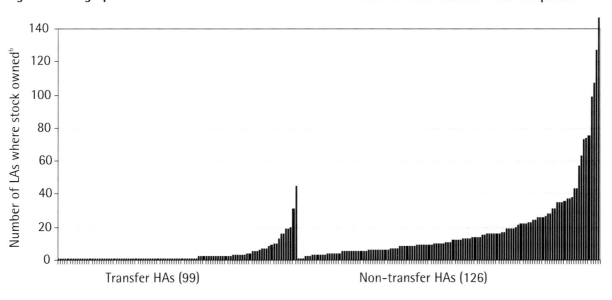

Notes: [a]The 225 largest 'mainly general needs' HAs as at April. [b]Excluding those containing less than 10 dwellings.
Source: The Housing Corporation regulatory and statistical returns (2001)

didn't vote [at transfer] for expanding into other areas", while the current ('independent') board chair felt that such moves were highly probable given the association's need to develop so as to counteract stock losses from sitting tenant sales. The association chief executive, meanwhile, viewed geographical diversification as highly unlikely in the foreseeable future "unless we are actually driven away by the [home] council". A related view is that closely contested transfers are liable to give rise to LA commitments to ensure that the transfer HA's development activities are locally focused (although there have been only a few instances of transfer HAs being bound by 'local-only development' covenants).

Nature of new housing development

In the main, new dwellings developed by transfer HAs have tended to be social rented housing. As shown in Figure 6, this is particularly true of the most recently created cohort of associations in England and has also been especially dominant in Scotland. Social rented housing also dominates transfer HAs' new development activities in home LAs. In England, for example, only 10% of transfer landlords' 'home LA' development has been for low-cost sale or shared ownership, while such schemes have accounted for 38% of activity in other areas. It may be that this reflects the delivery of undertakings to founding LAs that have a strong preference for the construction of social rented rather than Low Cost Home Ownership dwellings.

Functional diversification

Increasingly in recent years, central government and its regulatory bodies (The Housing Corporation and Communities Scotland) have been encouraging HAs to consider adopting a broader approach to housing management and/or to take on 'community regeneration' activities well beyond the traditional landlord role (for example, Scottish Homes, 2000). Partly in response to such signals, nearly 1 in 10 English HAs (owning more than 750 homes) was, by 2000/01, engaged in 'non-housing' activities accounting for more than 5% of its turnover (The Housing Corporation regulatory statistical returns data, 2001).

On The Housing Corporation's 'diverse activities' measure, transfer associations do not appear to be in the vanguard of the 'housing plus' movement: only 1 in 20 is engaged in 'non-housing' pursuits valued at more than 5% of its turnover. Many are, nevertheless, moving into such areas. Other than the Corporation's encouragement, there are two main drivers for such moves: first, the need to respond to LA aspirations, and second, associations' own ambitions to seek imaginative ways of 'growing their business'.

Particularly among partial transfer HAs, LAs are increasingly investing new landlords with specific obligations to promote 'community regeneration' with respect to the transferred stock and its

Figure 6: Type of new housing developed by transfer HAs

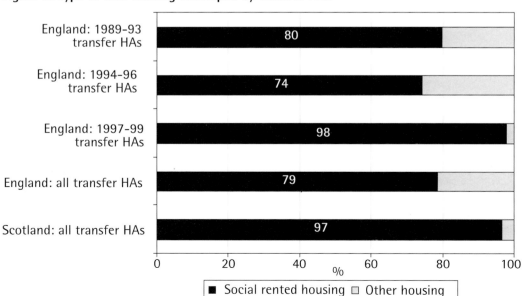

residents. Charlton Triangle Homes, for example, has delivered skills training, as well as running summer play schemes and counselling for single parents. Other activities undertaken in pursuit of these 'housing plus' objectives have included the provision of after-school clubs, employment training and crime prevention (Perry, 2002). Nearly a quarter of English transfer HAs reported in our postal survey that they were obliged to undertake such activities by clauses in their transfer contracts.

As our postal survey evidence demonstrates, most transfer HAs in England are experienced in 'housing plus' activities of one kind or another (see Table 16). This is true of longer-established and more recently set-up associations in roughly equal measure. Community facilities developed by transfer HAs often involve day centres, training suites, tenants' meeting areas and the like. While there are no directly comparable figures for non-transfer associations, these numbers seem to contradict the impression conveyed by the Corporation's 'diverse activities' measure (see above) that transfer HAs are relatively uninvolved in such pursuits. The generally lower activity rates in Scotland probably reflect the relatively small size (and more limited resources) of transfer HAs here.

Business-oriented diversification has rather different implications. It may, for example, involve seeking to deploy an association's existing development expertise in new (non-housing) contexts. Bedfordshire Pilgrims HA, for example, has recently entered into a partnership to provide care home establishments to be run by a specialist provider. This field was also seen as a potential area for expansion by other case study landlords.

Whatever its precise nature, functional diversification cuts across the argument that, as single-purpose bodies, transfer HAs are able to

operate in a more single-minded way than a LA landlord.

Moving into surplus

Since the mid-1990s, operating conditions have tended to become more challenging for HAs. Low or falling inflation and rising works tender costs have been accompanied by increasingly strict rent controls. While the difficulties caused for certain landlords due to rent restructuring have generated considerable debate, The Housing Corporation's earlier introduction of guideline rents is seen as having been a more significant move for associations collectively.

Some longer-established transfer landlords have found it necessary to generate revenue savings through measures such as centralisation, sometimes in the context of group structures (see Chapter 3). However, while many of them have also found it possible to take advantage of the low interest rate environment to refinance their operations[10], this option is open only to associations which have outperformed business plan projections and secured the confidence of lenders. Usually, such refinancing takes place on the back of increased borrowing facilities where the association is taking on more debt to finance new development, allowing the lender to offer reduced rates over a larger total debt, so enabling an association to escape from the straight-jacket of high rate loans taken on in the early 1990s. One case study HA from this era had, for example, found it possible to reduce its average interest rate from 14% to 7% in this way. At the same time, the association's strong record

---

[10] It is reported that "the majority of financially strong [HAs] receiving good quality stock refinanced their loan facilities within the first two to three years after their transfer" (Ernst and Young, 2002, cited in NAO, 2003, p 28).

Table 16: 'Housing plus' activities of transfer HAs

Activity	England	Scotland
Developed community facilities	71	40
Community development or capacity building	58	13
Skills training for local residents	62	20
Budgeting/money advice (other than in connection with rent arrears)	20	13
Established credit union	20	20
Summer play schemes	38	7

Table 17: Transfer HAs set up before April 1999: period from transfer to peak debt

| Jurisdiction | Years from set-up until peak debt | | | | | Total responding HAs |
	<6	6–9	10–13	14–17	18+	
England	4	9	10	9	5	37
Scotland	0	2	3	3	2	10

enabled it to negotiate new loans on more flexible terms – previously inflexible covenants prohibiting cross-subsidy between schemes, for example, were dropped.

In the longer term, provided that business plans do not come completely unstuck, most transfer landlords can look forward to developing a very strong financial position as they pass their peak debt year (see Table 17). For some of the HAs concerned, the structure of their original financing means that peak debt may be passed within five years of transfer. For others, it is not projected until as late as Year 27.

Postal survey evidence suggests that around a quarter of the 100 transfer HAs established in England before April 1999 have, by 2003, passed their peak debt year. By 2005 a third will have done so. Some landlords having passed peak debt see this as enabling them to alter their focus through becoming more active in community regeneration activities such as the construction of community facilities, the establishment of employment and training initiatives and so on.

For transfer HAs themselves, and perhaps for their tenants, peak debt year marks the threshold of a more favourable financial position. Activities such as landbanking to facilitate future development may become possible.

The perceived significance of passing peak debt year varies from association to association. Responding in our postal survey, one long-established association, for example, reported that passing their peak debt year "had a profound cultural effect. We stopped thinking of ourselves as an LSVT and started seeking loan funding comparable with that of other RSLs". Other respondents doubted that passing peak debt would have any impact on their association's activities (in some cases because periodic refinancing and a large development programme reduced the significance of the event). The prevailing view, however, was that

passing peak debt would or has facilitated the expansion of housing development and/or functional diversification.

To the extent that post-peak debt surpluses are ploughed back into housing and other community regeneration investment, national policy objectives may be furthered as a result. At the same time, however, central government has no leverage enabling it to compel post-peak debt HAs to make use of revenue surpluses in this way or, more radically, to redistribute such surpluses to reflect the distribution of housing need. Particularly given that the transferred stock is a publicly funded asset, this could be seen as a flaw in the transfer model (HACAS Consulting, 1999; Malpass and Mullins, 2002). Similarly, the National Audit Office has suggested that transfer valuations have often tended to undervalue transferring stock partly because of not factoring in the residual value after a 30-year life (NAO, 2003). Likewise, the official discount rate used in the transfer valuation model has historically been fixed at a rate substantially in excess of the real cost of capital in recent years. Again, this has led to 'undervaluation'[11].

With central government's recent decision to reform aspects of the transfer valuation model, it may be that transfer associations created in the future will not come to resemble their longer-established counterparts in terms of the long-term potential for generating financial surpluses. For most currently existing transfer landlords, however, long-run prospects appear to be fairly rosy.

---

[11] For example, the National Audit Office estimated that the value placed on one transfer would have been more than 50% higher if the discount rate had reflected the actual cost of capital as subsequently experienced (NAO, 2003, p 4).

8

Relationships with local authorities

Introduction

In England, at least, all stock transfer HAs have been founded by LAs which have, in some cases, seen them as bodies potentially susceptible to their continuing influence. Constitutionally, however, transfer landlords are independent organisations that are in no way subservient to their LA founders. Some transfer HAs may be contractually obliged to honour certain specific obligations laid down by their 'home LA' in transfer agreements. Generally, however, the nature of such relationships does not fit within the central–local relations model, but is characteristic of the looser-knit 'network' interactions identified by Reid (1995) as assuming increasing importance in the social housing sphere.

This chapter looks at the nature of relationships between founding LAs and transfer landlords, at the tensions that sometimes attend such relationships, and at the way such relationships develop over time. It also refers to the relationships between transfer HAs and other bodies with whom they interact.

LAs and transfer HAs – a special relationship?

Transfer landlords, like other HAs, are encouraged by their regulators to assert their independence. In England, nearly half of them have also expanded the geographical scope of their activities beyond their original founding LA. Nevertheless, in England at least, the vast majority still consider themselves to enjoy a 'special relationship' with that authority (see Table 18). Interestingly, this is just as true of those set up in 1988-96 as those more recently established.

The finding that only one Scottish transfer association considers its relationship with its 'home LA' to be 'special' should probably not be regarded as surprising. It reflects the fact that these organisations were not created by LAs. These associations also differ from most of their English counterparts in that they do not stand out as dominant players in terms of the proportion of social housing stock managed in a particular authority. In this respect, they are more like the English partial transfer landlords – few of whom consider that their relationship with their home authority is 'special' (see Table 18). It may well be that the status of (most of) these

Table 18: Relationship with 'home LA' (%)

Is there a 'special relationship' with the 'home LA'?	England				Scotland
	Whole stock transfers		Partial		
	1988-96	1997-99	transfers	All	
Yes	82	82	17	73	8
No	18	18	83	27	92
Total	100	100	100	100	100
Number of respondents	28	11	6	45	13

Table 19: English whole stock transfer landlords: features of 'special relationship' with 'home LA' (%)

Features of 'special relationship'	1988-96	1997-99	All
More frequent/regular bilateral officer-level contacts between the parties	61	45	56
Greater interest in the HA's activities on the part of LA members	75	82	77
Greater expectations of the HA on the part of the 'home LA'	71	73	72
Greater interest on the part of the 'home LA' in HA strategic decisions	75	73	74
Qualitatively greater involvement of the HA in the LA's strategic housing policy making	61	55	59
Nominations arrangements which differ from most other local HAs	50	55	51
Financial benefits to HA, eg share of reinvested transfer capital receipt	43	27	38
Other	4	0	3
No special relationship	18	18	18
Number of respondents	28	11	39

organisations as subsidiaries within HA groups influences their primary loyalties.

As demonstrated by Table 19, there appear to be a number of largely standard aspects to the special relationship between transfer HAs and their 'home authorities'. Compared with their non-transfer counterparts, for example, most English transfer HAs continue to be regarded with greater interest by LAs and subject to more challenging expectations. 'First among equals' might describe this position. Generally, there is little difference between first wave and more recently established transfer landlords in terms of the perceived significance of the various aspects of the special relationship.

A 'common-sense' explanation of perceived 'special relationships' might be that this is mainly due to the typical pre-eminence of a transfer landlord in terms of being the largest social landlord operating in its locality. Another factor, as already discussed in Chapter 5, is that most founding LAs retain representation on the transfer HA boards (something which is believed to be relatively unusual in the respect of 'traditional' HAs). Case study and other evidence, however, confirms that there is usually much more to the story than this. In particular, many transfer landlords remain functionally integrated with their founding LAs in ways that are quite distinct from the relationships between councils and non-transfer HAs.

Functional integration

Functional integration of this sort often involves transfer associations having both client and contractor liaison with their LA counterpart. For example, about half of all whole stock transfer landlords in England manage housing registers and/or homelessness assessment on behalf of their home LA (Pawson and Mullins, 2003). Such contracts usually run for five-year terms, after which they may be retendered. Their establishment often reflects a LA view that the management of access to housing is an integral element of housing management. It can also stem from a council's wish to minimise its post-transfer operational involvement in housing activities. Sometimes this can reflect an inaccurate perception that, through outsourcing a function such as homelessness assessment, the council sheds all responsibility for the discharge of this service. Another impetus may be the wish of a former LA housing director, appointed as chief executive of the transfer HA and seeking to retain control of all their former responsibilities.

Where contracts for functions of this sort are taken on by transfer HAs, this does not always reflect a positive aspiration on the part of the association concerned: sometimes it accedes only reluctantly to a strongly expressed expectation on the council's part. Such reluctance may reflect a view that taking on such functions limit an association's independence (or, at least, its perceived independence).

Some transfer HAs contract services *from* their home LA counterparts. One 'first-wave' case study landlord, for example, has continued to use its local council's direct labour organisation as one of its repairs contractors – even after more than a decade. This relationship, which has come to account for around half of the HA's repairs spend, is on a purely business footing and has been subject to a number of tendering exercises over the post-transfer period. Other council services sometimes provided to transfer landlords under contract include grounds maintenance and information technology.

Development funding

Another important component of many 'special relationships' between transfer HAs and founding LAs is the 'priority treatment' many of the former have been given in the distribution of LA Social Housing Grant (SHG). Openly preferential arrangements have tended to be particularly common in the first few years post-transfer (although their significance is obviously dependent on whether the transfer generates a net capital receipt). In the case of one early transfer HA, for example, the transfer agreement mandated the council to (a) provide £3 million in grant funding in Year 1, and (b) give the association 'priority of funding' for £10 million in Years 2-5. In practice, the association has continued to attract the greater part of the council's housing investment resources and, demonstrating the continuing strength of the relationship a decade after transfer, was allocated 100% of the LA's SHG in 2000/01 and 2001/02.

In the past, a transfer HA's wish to retain privileged access to LA SHG has provided a strong motivation for maintaining a positive relationship with its founding LA, even if this sometimes involves activities which are unattractive on strictly business terms. With the impending abolition of LA SHG, however, this particular incentive for transfer HAs to foster close relations with LAs will disappear.

Tensions with founding LAs

While strong relationships between transfer HAs and their founding LAs are often maintained over long periods, tensions between the parties are far from rare. To an extent, such stresses simply reflect the evolution of a relationship where the LA as the founding body has to 'learn to let go' of the new organisation and accept the reality of partnership rather than parenthood. In many instances, problems arising in the immediate post-transfer period reflect personal relationships and petty jealousies between former colleagues.

In particular, remaining LA staff are often envious of the better working conditions and/or conditions of employment experienced by their contemporaries who have switched across to the new body. Such resentments are often triggered by the HA's move to newly acquired or constructed offices, frequently more fit for purpose than accommodation occupied by local government staff.

Issues generic to relationships between LAs and HAs

Some of the other issues giving rise to relationship stress with transfer LAs, although perhaps larger in scale, may be little different in kind to those attending the interaction of LAs and traditional HAs. Such issues include:

- day-to-day operational liaison over issues such as nominations and Housing Benefit;
- LA funding of HA investment;
- perceived LA weakness on strategic housing policy making.

Day-to-day operational liaison

Day-to-day operational liaison frequently gives rise to strains over issues such as disputed nominations and Housing Benefit delays. These may assume particular significance because of a (whole stock) transfer HA's pre-eminent size, and, in the case of nominations, because they bear on the question of the HA's establishment of itself as an entity independent of its founding LA. A factor specific to some transfer HAs is the relatively high nomination entitlements typically agreed with LAs (Pawson and Mullins, 2003). Frustration at council performance on Housing Benefit may also be particularly keenly felt in recently established transfer HAs, reflecting the commonly experienced post-transfer shock at the changed relationship with Housing Benefit staff under the rent allowance (rather than rent rebate) framework. Generally, however, tensions of this sort are not significantly different in kind from those attending the relationship between LAs and non-transfer HAs.

LA funding of HA investment

Well over a third of English transfer HAs believe that access to LA capital funding is an aspect of

47

their special relationship with their founding council. An example of such 'favourable arrangements' has already been cited above. However, while such understandings may be built into transfer agreements, evidence suggests that, beyond the first few years of its existence, it is rare for a transfer HA to continue to enjoy such priority treatment 'as of right'. LAs, seeking to focus their development relationships, often undertake semi-competitive assessments of a range of potential 'preferred partners' so as to select a limited number with whom they will work particularly closely.

Although a transfer HA often enjoys a significant advantage in such assessments, complacency can be a mistake. In spite of its generally good relations with its founding LA, for example, one case study HA had been excluded from the LA's initial list of 'preferred partners' resulting from such an assessment. This decision, four years after transfer, aroused consternation, although the HA was subsequently successful in lobbying for the decision's reversal.

In another case study instance, transfer HA senior managers had understood from discussions prior to set-up that the organisation would have a privileged status in relation to its founding LA's distribution of SHG. Other HAs active in the district would be limited to resources from The Housing Corporation's Approved Development Programme (ADP). The council's post-transfer decision that meeting Best Value requirements necessitated an element of competition for SHG allocations led to resentment and mistrust on the association's part.

In Scotland there has traditionally been no equivalent of the LA SHG regime and, consequently, less incentive for transfer (or other) HAs to develop close relationships with them. However, some development funding, for example under Scottish Executive challenge funds, may be accessed by HAs through (rather than from) LAs. In spite of its non-LA origins, one of our case study HAs – WESLO – has developed strong links with LA partners and, as a result, has secured substantial resources to fund new development (see Chapter 7). Aspects of this close relationship included an unusually high nominations entitlement of 75%.

Perceived LA weakness on strategic housing policy making

A significant frustration experienced in many transfer associations is the difficulty presented by what is seen as an inadequate housing presence retained in the post-transfer LA. This sometimes results from a mistaken impression on the part of councils that ceasing to be a landlord brings to an effective end their housing responsibilities (Audit Commission, 2002). Not only is the number of retained 'housing' staff often very small but, lacking their own department, their corporate influence can be quite limited. In addition, there is the problem of 'intellectual asset-stripping' – the tendency for the lure of the transfer association to strip away all a housing department's most creative and dynamic staff. Where a post-transfer LA's retained housing capacity is inadequate, this can seriously inhibit the potential for constructive dialogue between it and its transfer HA partner.

Issues specific to relations between transfer HAs and LAs

In some cases, stresses between transfer HAs and home LAs relate to issues that are quite distinct from those that attend LA relationships with non-transfer associations. Case study evidence suggests that the most significant of such matters fall under the following headings:

- operational relationships relating to contracted functions;
- fallout from 'defective' HA business plans;
- HA growth ambitions.

Contractual relationships

Where services such as housing register management or homelessness assessment are carried out by a transfer HA under contract to its founding LA, tensions can arise from the frequently poor service specification and/or unrealistic fee structures involved. For example, one case study HA managing homelessness assessment under contract found itself under pressure to subsidise the service from its own resources because the contractor fee took no account of the 50% increase in homelessness presentations in the three years since the arrangement's inception. Frustrations on the LA side often reflect the failure of contracts to incorporate performance incentives, for example, to minimise the use of expensive temporary accommodation for homeless households.

Similar financially motivated concerns over their possible consequences for the rehousing of homeless households may also underlie LA scepticism at transfer HA proposals for policy innovations in the allocations field, for example, estate profiling or choice-based lettings.

The inadequacies of housing register management and homelessness assessment contracts are often attributed to the competing pressures faced by a LA in the immediate pre-transfer period, and there is evidence that 'second-generation' contracts for services of this kind are often more sophisticated (Pawson and Mullins, 2003).

Where a transfer landlord is a service client of its founding LA, there can be an assumption on the LA side that this relationship will be preserved for the foreseeable future, irrespective of performance or the possible advantages of switching to another contractor – or, indeed, HA in-house provision. One case study HA, for example, had provoked outrage among founding council members by opting for non-renewal of service-level agreements a year after transfer. The likelihood that a transfer HA will continue to contract services from its founding body is often a key factor influencing opinion as to the merits of a transfer proposal in the lead-up to the tenants' ballot. Furthermore, European Union (EU) competition rules now cast doubt on a council's powers to enforce such arrangements post-transfer. In the case of Dumfries and Galloway's planned (2003) transfer, for example, doubts were raised about the legality of an undertaking by the new landlord to contract repairs services from the council's direct labour organisation for a five-year period. Such was the perceived importance of the issue from the council's perspective that these uncertainties threatened to derail the entire proposal (in spite of its existing ballot endorsement by tenants) (Robertson, 2003).

Fallout from 'defective' HA business plans

Tensions are liable to arise from instances where a transfer HA finds that (with hindsight) over-

optimistic business plan assumptions necessitate economies in its operation. As noted in Chapter 7, problems of this kind are particularly likely to occur early in a transfer landlord's existence, in part because of the frequently imperfect nature of information available in advance of set-up. Proposed remedial action such as rephasing of refurbishment programmes, functional centralisation or withdrawal from 'community regeneration' activities are liable to be seen by founding LAs as a breach of transfer promises (or, at least, understandings).

The extent of the tensions to which such problems give rise is, of course, dependent on the extent to which a founding LA continues to maintain a sense of 'ownership' of the association involved. Evidence seems to suggest that this is liable to be particularly strong in the case of partial transfers – often seen by a LA as integral to its wider regeneration strategy. The challenging circumstances often faced by partial transfer HAs (see Chapter 4) also make them particularly vulnerable to financial and other difficulties.

Sometimes, disputes arise not because of the need to reshape an association's business plan, but because of LA members' inadequate appreciation of its original contents – or the contents reflect changed local circumstances post-transfer. In Coventry, for example, it was recently reported that councillors from across the political spectrum had condemned the transfer HA's plans to demolish 500 flats on a particular estate. In fact, the association's founding business plan had anticipated the clearance of 1,300 homes, albeit without specifying the exact location of these (*Housing Today*, 23 January 2003). Alternatively, it may have been that perceived post-transfer shifts in affordable housing demand in the city could have led councillors to believe that pre-transfer plans needed modification.

HA growth ambitions

It seems unlikely that many founding LAs would object to an association's aspiration for growth, particularly where this can be argued as beneficial in reducing unit overhead costs. However, when such ambitions involve expansion outside the boundaries of a transfer HA's home LA, tensions often arise. In particular, where such growth is to be facilitated through the development of group structures with other landlords, a founding LA may perceive its influence as being diluted. Evidence from one case study suggests that proposals for cross-collateralisation (where it is proposed that transferred stock may be used as security for another group member's borrowing) are particularly likely to prove controversial. In any event, official guidance relating to group structures in the transfer context now requires that "ownership of transferred stock should ... rest with the (group) subsidiary ... responsible for delivering the landlord function" (DTLR, 2001, p 177).

Evolving relationships in the longer term

To what extent do relationships between transfer HAs and founding LAs cool as the passage of time makes the specific origins of the new organisation more remote? Perhaps surprisingly, only just over a third (36%) of English transfer landlords – and none in Scotland – believed that relations had cooled since the immediate post-transfer period (see Table 20). This refers to a period of at least two years (since the sample included only landlords set up before April 1999). It is particularly interesting that only half of the 22 1988-96 transfer HAs believed that relations had become more distant since the immediate post-transfer period. Nine reported that relations remained unchanged or had grown closer over this period.

In interpreting Table 20 it should, however, be appreciated that the HA–LA relationship can be particularly fraught in the period immediately following transfer. A number of case study landlords reported that their respective home LAs

had initially found it difficult to come to terms with their association's independent status. One council, for example, was seen as having mistakenly envisaged its transfer 'offspring' as "an arm's-length subsidiary of the council.... [We] were divorced from the council but [it] thought we had just moved into the spare bedroom" (HA senior manager).

The Scottish results on this question are also interesting, bearing in mind the non-LA origins of these bodies. Eight of the 12 HAs responding here felt that they had become *more closely engaged* with their home LA since transfer.

Although transfer landlords and their LA founders can drift apart over time, the extent to which this occurs depends on a number of factors. These include:

- the personal inclinations of senior staff on both sides of the relationship;
- the extent to which the transfer association seeks to, or succeeds in, developing new housing outside its own area (see Chapter 7);
- the scale of the task faced by the landlord in renovating the inherited stock; and
- the degree to which the two organisations remain functionally integral.

Our case study transfer HAs included examples of instances where the association, having initially moved away from a focus on its home LA, later opted for a strategy of consolidation, recommitting itself to its original area, for example in terms of community regeneration investment. Even among the longest-established and most 'aggressive' 'out of area developers', a strong commitment to the founding LA often remains in place.

Table 20: Changes in relationships between transfer HAs and 'home LAs' (%)

By comparison with immediate post-transfer period, relationship with home LA is now ...	England				Scotland
	Whole stock transfers		Partial transfers	Total	
	1988-96	1997-99			
Closer	29	27	0	24	67
More distant	43	27	17	36	0
Neither closer nor more distant	29	45	83	40	33
Number of respondents	28	11	6	45	12

Note: Percentages may not add to 100 due to rounding.

9

Conclusions and policy implications

Conclusions

Since the late 1980s, stock transfer has been a catalyst for substantial change in the delivery of social housing services and in the management of social housing organisations. In part, this reflects the ability of transfer associations, properly set up, to access investment resources, but also derives from the fact that the post-transfer regime has tended to result in:

- a liberating effect on housing staff;
- the adoption of a more customer-focused approach to housing management;
- innovations in landlords' organisational structures and staff management practices in favour of more openness and more widespread ownership of corporate objectives.

Transfer often triggers genuine change in organisational ethos, summarised by staff interviewees in some of our case studies as replacing a 'no' culture with a 'yes' culture. The step change in available investment resources, the increased control over organisational destiny, and an increased sense of freedom from LA constraints underpins this transformation. Leadership is also important. The typically flatter structures adopted and the desire to make all staff more aware of organisational goals and constraints means that the leadership style and priorities can make a fundamental impact on the ethos of these new organisations. This impact is usually, although not invariably, highly positive.

In the early years following transfer, newly created landlords are often highly vulnerable to any misjudged assumptions contained in original business plans, as this is the time when expenditure commitments are large and explicit,

while the organisations are typically also highly indebted and becoming more so. In a transfer landlord's early years there is also substantial potential for conflicts at board level. The risk of discord within the governing body is exacerbated by the sectional basis of the local housing company model, leading to a 'constituency mentality' and tension between the board members 'representing' different interest groups. The initial effectiveness of board members is also undermined by the typically very short lead-in time from ballot decision to organisational set-up which allows relatively little opportunity for shadow board members to become accustomed to appropriate ways of working.

Over time, transfer associations evolve as social businesses, needing to react flexibly to changing external conditions while having to respect key business plan assumptions and targets. While there has been a tendency for longer-established transfer landlords to develop into 'regional players', this is not an inevitable trajectory for more recently created landlords. Indeed, there is reason to believe that many, if not most, transfer HAs created since 1996 will retain a local focus for the foreseeable future.

This underlines the scope for differentiation within the transfer sub-sector. More recently created organisations (groups II and III, as defined by Table 4, page 8) are generally operating from a less favourable base and will perhaps always have less scope than the most fortunate older organisations. Even within the same cohort (in terms of era of establishment), some, particularly in Scotland, have been content largely to act as good managers of their existing stock, while others have pursued higher risk strategies and more actively sought development opportunities locally and more widely.

Partly due to their need to accommodate common regulatory requirements, transfer landlords inevitably develop some similarities with 'traditional' HAs. And the growing emphasis on performance culture and customer orientation in social housing organisations more generally is strongly reflected in the operation of these landlords. Collectively, however, transfer HAs retain a number of distinctive features, for example:

- a stock profile which, in age, type and design, differs from that of most traditional associations;
- particularly close ties with founder LAs, either through functional integration, 'preferred development partner' status or the influence wielded at board level by councillor board members;
- substantial tenant participation in (although not necessarily influence over) governance (contrasting less significantly with traditional associations in Scotland than in England);
- a local focus to their activities differing from that of non-transfer associations of a comparable size;
- a growth imperative resulting from the contraction of stock due to the continuing impact of RTB sales;
- a longer-term potential to generate substantial surpluses which may be ploughed back into additional housing development or into non-housing 'community regeneration' style activities.

A number of these distinctive features are likely to remain present for the foreseeable future and, as transfer landlords begin to dominate the sector as a whole over the coming decade, they will be increasingly seen as typical of HAs per se.

In their scope for independent action, and their reliance on the quality of relationships with other bodies, notably LAs, the growing importance of transfer associations within the social housing sector is consistent with the body of theory which stresses the significance of interorganisational networks and negotiation rather than the central–local relations model (for example Mullins et al, 2001). As the Audit Commission has argued, scrutiny rather than control is likely to be the key mode of operation in the post-transfer governance of housing (Audit Commission, 2001, 2002).

Policy implications

This research has filled a significant gap in understanding of the contemporary housing scene – namely the nature and operation of the new landlords created by stock transfer. In contrast with the emphasis of previous studies, it has deliberately concentrated on the ways in which the new organisations differ from their predecessor bodies and, more importantly, how they change post-transfer. This also meant that the research needed to focus on organisations that are past the immediate post-transfer period and had been operating as a new, independent organisation for at least three years at the time of the fieldwork (2002).

Inevitably then, some of the evidence reflects on the rules and conditions that faced earlier generations of transfer organisations, some of which have subsequently changed (and which, in any case, have always differed between England and Scotland). The general direction of such change has tended to be towards greater regulation within a less favourable economic climate. At the same time, the councils now contemplating stock transfer are, by and large, seeking solutions for stock in poorer condition and with higher residual debts than was the case during the early years of the transfer programme. The sense of transfer marking an 'escape from the LA strait-jacket' into a more freewheeling existence is likely to be much less strongly felt among transfer associations set up in 2003 as compared to their early 1990s counterparts.

In drawing conclusions from this work we are, nevertheless, able to identify some general lessons to be drawn from the earlier transfers that could inform future practice in managing both transfers and the landlords created through the process. More widely, some of our findings have implications for the setting up and operation of Arm's-Length Management Organisations (ALMOs) increasingly being seen (in England) as an alternative to full-blown transfer.

A sense of realism about the transfer option

Some of the tensions often experienced in the relationship between LAs and transfer HAs, particularly in the initial post-transfer period, result from unrealistic councillor assumptions that the new body remains susceptible to council control as well as influence. Transfer advocates may feel that winning council members' approval for their plans necessitates the maintenance of ambiguity in this area. Such an approach, however, complicates the task of managing the post-transfer HA and can lead to a long-term souring of relations. A more open approach would seek to generate a greater sense of understanding and ownership of the decision on the part of members and facilitate a stronger footing for constructive post-transfer relationships between the parties. Similarly, as the National Audit Office has observed, there is a need for transfer pledges on matters such as property upgrading to be clear and specific (NAO, 2003, p 17).

Registration rules

Some of the benefits of transfer have clearly derived from the fact that it has generated organisations which are not only single-purpose, but also much smaller and more self-contained than their LA (or Scottish Homes) predecessors. In England, at least, this outcome has been shaped significantly by the maximum size of transfer HA rules (5,000 dwellings, later relaxed to 12,000) which have been enforced through the registration process. There must be legitimate concerns as to whether such benefits will be realised where larger LAs transfer into group structure-type arrangements which may bear at least a passing resemblance to the predecessor LA headquarters and district office framework. Do the subsidiary landlords in this scenario have any genuine independence or sense of a distinct identity?

More importantly, concerns may be raised at the recent Office of the Deputy Prime Minister announcement (ODPM, 2003, p 42) that the 12,000 limit has been entirely removed. The overriding importance of facilitating achievement of decent homes targets must, of course, be acknowledged, and it may be that some larger LAs will be more amenable to the transfer option if assured that this can be achieved while retaining the unitary structure of their existing housing service[12]. At the same time, however, it is important that official policy in this area should

not lose sight of the advantages which have flowed from creating landlord bodies of a manageable size. 'Second-stage' transfers, whereby parcels of stock are handed on by a first-stage transfer landlord to smaller, locally based bodies, are of course one means by which this may be achieved (as envisaged in Glasgow).

Governance and the transfer process

There is clear evidence that, in their early years, transfer HAs are at risk of ineffective board governance and may face particular difficulty in holding management to account. Both independent and tenant board members often feel disadvantaged by their lack of knowledge of the subject area and/or experience relevant to their new role. Councillor nominees, on the other hand, often have an inappropriate conception of their function as members of the new body. While much effort is already expended in constituting and training shadow boards in the lead up to transfer, this process is often severely constrained by the tight timescale from ballot to stock handover. Unless it is considered appropriate to begin establishing a shadow board in advance of the ballot, there is a strong case for extending this timescale while, at the same time, committing more resources to pre-transfer board member recruitment and training.

Pre-transfer training for board members also needs to be more tailored. While 'whole group' sessions are essential for the development of cohesion and corporate identity, the typically disparate training needs of designate members from the three constituencies also call for more customised sessions.

In the selection of council nominees to transfer HA boards, the regulatory bodies need to emphasise more strongly the essentially non-political nature of HA board operation and the corollary that nominee selection should not be overly influenced by a perceived need for appropriate 'political balance'. Knowledge of, interest in, and commitment to resolving housing issues should be the main criteria for selection and councils should be encouraged more strongly to consider potential nominees outwith currently sitting council members. Where a post-

---

[12] And, in any case, registration rules influencing organisational size at start-up do nothing to prevent subsequent takeovers resulting in the creation of larger organisations whose centre of gravity may be geographically remote.

transfer council is 'represented' by, for example, ex-councillors or senior staff, there is a stronger likelihood of continuity and commitment. Councils should also be strongly discouraged from including their transfer HA representation within annual reviews of nominees to outside bodies. Ideally, nominees should be selected on three-year terms.

Another scenario common to the transfer process and which ought to provide pointers for the future is the nature of certain ballot undertakings. While there is an understandable need to provide tenants with assurance of 'improved housing management', this has often tended to be linked with specific commitments to a generic, area-based style of activity. Pledges of this kind may be seen as essential in demonstrating the seriousness of such undertakings and consistent with the aim of reducing pre-transfer ambiguity (see above). Evidence from existing transfer HAs, however, suggests that transfer planners should be wary of commitments of this kind because of their potential 'sacred cow' status in the post-transfer era. Maintaining a relatively underused network of local offices, for example, can be a costly liability for a transfer landlord.

Managing transfer HAs

There seems little evidence to support Cope's early prediction that transfer HAs would retain the bureaucratic habits of their LA predecessors (Cope, 1990, p 295). As they become more established, however, such tendencies may creep back into play. There is a particular danger that the structures set up to facilitate expansion, for example group arrangements, may recreate some of the inflexible and unwieldy hierarchies common to the council sector. Transfer HA managers (and their ALMO counterparts) need to seek ways of building on and maintaining the momentum created by the transfer process, and building participative organisational structures which retain the benefits of this experience.

Another danger is that the need to preserve an appearance of 'local identity', for example, as a group subsidiary, may create unjustifiable organisational complexity. Again, the potential for the recreation of a highly bureaucratic body needs to be guarded against.

Many transfer HAs have made good use of their relative freedom to explore the transferability of 'private sector' management techniques to a non-profit organisational setting. At the same time, however, there is evidence that some of these approaches have been, in many instances, found to be inappropriate and discarded. An important example concerns performance-related pay systems. There is a lesson here for transfer HAs (and, perhaps, ALMOs) created in the future: becoming a business-like organisation should not involve the uncritical adoption of market sector approaches.

Regulating transfer HAs

While regulation of transfer HAs is clearly essential to provide comfort to LAs, to funders and to tenants, there may be questions as to whether the regulatory burden now faced by all HAs is becoming onerous and excessive. Specifically in relation to transfer HAs, there is a need to retain some of the attractions of the HA operating context so as to preserve some of the incentives for transfer which motivated many of the earlier transfer councils. Through its moves towards a more graduated system of regulation and inspection, based on the assessed degree of organisational risk, as well as through its move away from the highly prescriptive 'Performance Standards' approach (Housing Corporation, 2002), The Housing Corporation is, in any case, moving in this direction.

At the same time, the growing recognition that many transfer HAs will, in time, come to generate large revenue surpluses underlies the National Audit Office's justifiable call for The Housing Corporation to seek ways of influencing how such surpluses are used "to ensure that [their deployment] support(s) overall government aims to improve social housing provision and develop sustainable communities" (NAO, 2003, p 29).

References

Audit Commission (2001) *A healthy outlook: Local authority overview and scrutiny of health*, London: Audit Commission.

Audit Commission (2002) *Housing services after stock transfer*, London: Audit Commission.

Audit Commission and Housing Corporation, The (2001) *Group dynamics: Group structures and registered social landlords*, London: Audit Commission and The Housing Corporation.

Cobbold, C. and Dean, J. (2000) *Views on the large scale voluntary transfer process*, London: DETR.

Cope, H. (1990) *Housing associations: Policy and practice*, London: Macmillan.

DETR (Department of the Environment, Transport and the Regions) (2000) *Quality and choice: The Housing Green Paper*, London: DETR.

DTLR (Department for Transport, Local Government and the Regions) (2001) *Housing transfer guidance 2002 programme*, London: DTLR.

Ernst and Young (2002) *Sources of finance for stock transfers*, London: Office of the Deputy Prime Minister.

Gardiner, K., Hills, J. and Kleinman, M. (1991) *Putting a price on council housing: Valuing voluntary transfers*, Welfare State Discussion Paper No 62, London: London School of Economics and Political Science.

Graham, T. (1997) *Transfers of local authority and Scottish Homes housing: A study of tenant and staff attitudes*, Edinburgh: Scottish Office Central Research Unit.

Graham, T. (1999) *An evaluation of Scottish Homes large scale voluntary transfers*, Research Report 75, Edinburgh: Scottish Homes.

HACAS Consulting (1999) *Housing associations: A viable financial future?*, Coventry: Chartered Institute of Housing.

Hartley, J. and Rashman, L. (2002) 'Organisational design in housing', Community Housing Task Force Discussion Paper No. 1, www.housing.odpm.gov.uk/chtf/pdf/discussion1.pdf

Holder, A., McQuillan, W., Fitzgeorge-Butler, A. and Williams, P. (1998) *Surviving or thriving? Managing change in housing organisations*, Coventry: Chartered Institute of Housing.

Housing Corporation, The (1998a) *Guidance for applicants seeking to become registered social landlords: Stock transfer applicants*, London: The Housing Corporation.

Housing Corporation, The (1998b) *No time to lose! Key issues for board members of startup transfer organisations*, London: The Housing Corporation.

Housing Corporation, The (2001) *Modernising governance*, London: The Housing Corporation.

Housing Corporation, The (2002) *The way forward: Our approach to regulatio*n, London: The Housing Corporation.

Jacobs, K. and Manzi, T. (2000) 'Performance indicators and social constructivism: conflict and control in housing management', *Critical Social Policy*, vol 62, pp 85-103.

Kearns, A. (1997) 'Housing association committees: dilemmas of composition', in P. Malpass (ed) *Ownership, control and accountability: The new governance of housing*, Coventry: Chartered Institute of Housing.

Malpass, P. (2000) *Housing associations and housing policy: A historical perspective*, London: Macmillan.

Malpass, P. and Mullins, D. (2002) 'Local authority housing stock transfer in the UK: from local initiative to national policy', *Housing Studies*, vol 17, no 4, pp 673-86.

Mullins, D. (1996) *Us and them: Report of a survey of housing enabling officers in local authorities which have transferred their housing stock under large scale voluntary transfers*, Birmingham: Centre for Urban and Regional Studies, University of Birmingham.

Mullins, D. and Riseborough, M. (2000) *What are housing associations becoming?*, Birmingham: School of Public Policy, University of Birmingham.

Mullins, D., Niner, P. and Riseborough, M. (1992) *Evaluating large scale voluntary transfers of local authority housing: Interim report*, London: HMSO.

Mullins, D., Niner, P. and Riseborough, M. (1995) *Evaluating large scale voluntary transfers of local authority housing*, London: HMSO.

Mullins, D., Reid, B. and Walker, R.M. (2001) 'Modernisation and change in social housing: the case for an organisational perspective', *Public Administration*, vol 79, no 3, pp 599-623.

NAO (National Audit Office) (2003) *Improving social housing through transfer: Report by the Comptroller and Auditor General*, London: The Stationery Office.

NHF (National Housing Federation) (2002a) *Why go to an existing housing association for transfer?*, Transfers to Transform Briefing No 2, London: NHF.

NHF (2002b) *Action for better homes: 14 years of stock transfer success*, London: NHF.

ODPM (Office of the Deputy Prime Minister) (2002) 'Housing statistics', at www.odpm.gov.uk/stellent/groups/ odpm_control/documents/

ODPM (2003) *Housing transfer manual: 2003 programme*, London: ODPM.

Pawson, H. and Mullins, D. (2003) *Changing places: Housing association policy and practice on nominations and lettings*, Bristol: The Policy Press.

Perry, J. (2002) 'Taking stock: partial transfers can play a key role in urban regeneration', *Housing*, September, pp 34-5.

PIEDA (1997) *Evaluation of the performance of large scale voluntary transfer housing associations*, PIEDA plc.

Pollitt, C., Birchall, J., and Putman, K. (1998) *Decentralising public sector management*, London: Macmillan.

Reid, B. (1995) Interorganisational networks and the delivery of local housing services, *Housing Studies*, vol 10, no 2, pp 133-49.

Reid, B. (2003: forthcoming) *Stock transfer HA tenant board members study*.

Robertson, D. (2003) 'It will cost the same as two Millennium Domes but will the stock transfer make any difference?', *Sunday Herald*, 9 February .

Rochester, C. and Hutchison, R. (2002) *Board effectiveness in transfer organisations*, London: National Housing Federation.

Scott, S., Currie, H., Fitzpatrick, S., Keoghan, M., Kintrea, K., Pawson, H. and Tate, J. (2001) *Good practice in housing management: A review of progress*, Edinburgh: Scottish Executive.

Scottish Homes (2000) 'Group structures including non-RSLs and related organisations', Scottish Homes Guidance Note SHGN 2000/08.

Scottish Office (1999) *Investing in modernisation: An agenda for Scotland's housing*, Green Paper, Edinburgh: The Stationery Office.

Taper, T., Walker, S. and Skinner, G. (2003) *LSVTs: Staff impacts and implications*, London: Office of the Deputy Prime Minister.

Taylor, M. (1998) 'Ten years of stock transfer', in S. Wilcox (ed) *Scottish Housing Review, 1988-1998*, Edinburgh: Scottish Homes.

Taylor, M. (2000) *Stock transfer past and present: A summary of research evidence*, Research Review No 6, Edinburgh: Scottish Homes.

Taylor, M. (2001) Database of Scottish stock transfers prepared for Scottish Executive (unpublished).

Walker, R. (1998) 'New public management and housing associations: from comfort to competition?', *Policy & Politics*, vol 26, no 1, pp 71-87.

Walker, R.M. (2000) 'The changing management of social housing: the impact of externalisation and managerialisation', *Housing Studies*, vol 15, no 2, pp 281-99.

Walker, R.M. (2001) 'How to abolish public sector housing: housing implications and lessons from public management reform, *Housing Studies*, vol 6, no 5, pp 675-96.

Wilcox, S., Bramley, G., Ferguson, A., Perry, J. and Woods, C. (1993) *Local housing companies: New opportunities for council housing*, York and London: Joseph Rowntree Foundation and Institute of Housing.

Appendix: Methodology

Postal survey of transfer landlords

Sample

A postal survey of transfer landlords in England and Scotland was carried out in February/March 2002. This covered all HAs specifically created for the purpose of taking on former LA, Scottish Homes or Scottish New Town housing stock and which:

- had been established before 1 April 1999;
- were managing more than 750 homes in 2001.

This amounted to 106 landlords in all. This sample broke down as follows:

- England: total sample 83 (72 whole stock transfer and 11 partial transfer bodies);
- Scotland: total sample 23 (1 former LA transfer, 1 former New Town transfer, 21 former Scottish Homes transfers).

Questionnaire

Recognising the significant differences in the institutional context between England and Scotland, two slightly differing versions of the questionnaire were used.

Response rates

In all, 61 responses were received – an overall response rate of 58%. This figure, generated through two chase-up mailings and direct phone calls, is fairly modest by comparison with response rates achieved in other recent postal surveys of social landlords we have carried out.

The relatively low figure achieved here is probably due to:

- the current level of research overload on LSVT HAs in England (see below); and
- the explicit requirement for our questionnaire to be completed by the chief executive or another senior manager with experience of the transfer process.

Indeed, we received a substantial number of letters from chief executives apologising for non-response. However, response rates were very similar for all the most significant sub-categories of landlord:

- Scottish HAs (65%), English HAs (55%);
- English partial transfers (55%), English whole stock transfers (55%)
- pre-1992 landlords (52%), 1992-95 landlords (60%), post-1995 landlords (59%).

On this basis, the achieved sample can be seen as fairly representative.

Case studies

A series of detailed case studies formed a key element of the project. In all, 12 case studies were carried out, nine in England and three in Scotland.

Purpose of case studies

The postal survey provided a comprehensive overview of how transfer landlords in England and Scotland are structured in terms of management and staffing, organisational culture and governance arrangements and the wider roles they play in local housing systems. Case studies were intended to facilitate probing of some of these issues in much greater detail. In particular, the aims of the case studies were to:

- facilitate a wider discourse of the ways in which LSVT landlords have responded to their new roles to date;
- provide different perspectives in terms of organisational culture and how it is changing in LSVT organisations.
- illustrate the impact of funding differences on housing management and practice;
- identify what factors are creating the most significant challenges faced by LSVT landlords;
- provide a more in-depth knowledge and understanding of the transfer process and its consequences for the housing system.

Case study selection

The most basic eligibility criterion was that the organisation needed to have responded to the postal survey. As well as providing certain key data which would inform our approach to each individual case study, this was also seen as indicating some engagement with the research on the part of the senior manager involved. Given that the postal survey drew 61 responses – 46 English and 15 Scottish HAs – this constituted our initial pool of landlords potentially eligible for case study selection.

Of the 46 English landlords potentially 'in the frame', 17 had recently been selected as case studies in other national projects. Hence, in selecting the nine English HAs for this project, we were limited to a field of just 29. The equivalent proportion for Scotland is three from 15.

Within this framework, we aimed to select a diverse group of transfer HAs in relation to:

- era of set-up;
- type of transfer (partial or whole stock);
- extent of expansion beyond initial LA;
- perceived relationship with 'home LA';
- whether or not the case study HA is in a group structure.

In the case of Scotland we were also interested to include both registered and non-registered landlords. The actual sample chosen is shown in Table 21.

Case study work

In the main, the case study work involved in-depth interviews with the various stakeholders, that is:

- transfer HA chief executive and senior managers;
- transfer HA middle manager and junior staff;
- transfer HA tenant 'representatives' (for example board members);
- (other) transfer HA board members;
- LA staff responsible for housing strategy/HA liaison;
- LA members with an interest in housing and/ or represented on the HA board.

In selecting potential interviewees, those with a longstanding involvement with social housing in the locality were prioritised.

Where possible we also consulted the relevant regional office of The Housing Corporation to obtain their view on how case study HAs had developed since their establishment and how this compared with other transfer landlords in the region.

A topic guide was developed as a structure for these interviews. These were set out within a structure similar to that used for the postal survey questionnaire:

- background to the original transfer;
- HA management structure and organisational culture;
- HA governance arrangements and how these have developed since transfer;
- HA housing management, development and diversification;
- relationships between HA and other organisations, particularly the 'home LA';
- likely future developments.

Under each of these headings, we sought to understand the current situation, the situation immediately following transfer and how – and why – things had changed over the intervening period.

Documents

In addition to the interviews, case study work also involved detailed scrutiny of relevant documents. These included transfer contracts, business plans and similar papers. For the longer-established landlords, there was an emphasis on assessing the continuity or evolution of objectives and strategic direction.

Write-up and feedback

Drawing on the interviews and the documents, we produced a draft working paper for each case study landlord and fed this back to the main informants so that content could be checked for accuracy and comprehensiveness.

Table 21: Case study HAs

Association	Jurisdiction	Home LA	Era of establishment	Type	Region	Size	Group structure?
Bedfordshire Pilgrims	England	Bedford	Early	W	E	Large	No
Charlton Triangle	England	Greenwich	Late	P	London	Small	Established as group subsidiary
Derwent & Solway	England	Allerdale	Late	W	NW	Medium	No
Hereward	England	East Cambridgeshire	Mid	W	E	Large	No
Knowes	Scotland	West Dunbartonshire	Late	P	W Scotland	Medium	No
Leasowe	England	Wirral	Late	P	NW	Small	Established as group subsidiary
Linx	England	East Lincolnshire	Late	W	Y&H	Medium	No
Manor Estates	Scotland	Edinburgh	Mid	P	E Scotland	Small	No
Severn Vale	England	Tewksbury	Late	W	SW	Medium	No
South Somerset	England	South Somerset	Late	W	SW	Large	No
Suffolk Heritage	England	Suffolk Coastal	Early	W	E	Large	Recently formed group structure
Weslo	Scotland	West Lothian	Mid	P	E Scotland	Small	No

Notes:

Era of establishment: Early = 1989-93, Mid = 1994-97, Late = 1998-99.

Type: W = whole stock, P = partial stock (ex-Scottish Homes transfers treated as partials).

Size: Small = less than 2,000; Medium = 2,000-6,000; Large = more than 6,000.